Learning Disabilities

How to Recognize and Manage Learning and Behavioral Problems in Children

by

Trudy Carlson

First Edition

Benline Press
Duluth, Minnesota

Copyright 1997 by Trudy Carlson M.S.

ISBN 09642443-2-2 Library of Congress No. 95-94110

All rights reserved. No part of this book may be reproduced or utilized in any form or by any means, electronic or mechanical, including photocopying, recording or by any information storage and retrieval system, without permission in writing from the publisher. For information address:

Benline Press, 118 N. 60th Avenue East
Duluth, Minnesota 55804

Publisher's Cataloging in Publication Data
Carlson, Trudy M.
Learning Disabilities: How to Recognize and Manage
Learning and Behavioral Problems in Children
Includes bibliographical references and Index
1. Attention-deficit hyperactivity disorder.
2. Attention-deficit hyperactivity disorder--Treatment.
3. Attention-deficit-disordered children.
4. Attention-deficit-disordered children--Education.
5. Dyslexia.
RJ506.H9   618.92/8589   95-94110
096424432-2-2

Praise for Learning Disabilities from:

Teachers
"I feel Trudy Carlson's first-hand account of her son's struggle with ADD should be on the recommended reading list of teacher training institutions. I certainly wish it had been available for me."
Ms. Jo Stewart, M.S. English Teacher and Speech Coach

"As a first grade teacher, I have read many articles and books on ADHD. Trudy's book is the most insightful and informative book I have read on the subject. It is a much needed resource which parents and teachers can use for identifying and helping these youngsters."*Margaret Kinetz, Elementary Teacher*

"A well-written and insightful look into the life of one child with ADHD. I suspect that many parents would benefit from the research and personal story that Trudy presents in this book. Teachers should be required to read this account before they are placed in classrooms."
Robin Blatnik, M.A.E.S. English and Composition Instructor

Parents
"This is a wonderful book to open the eyes of anyone who reads it. It is an important start to raising the awareness of the connection between ADHD and depression, as well as giving insight into dyslexia." *Monica Natzel, mother of a youngster with ADHD*

"This is practical, from-the-trenches information that could change the lives of so many kids! Too many youngsters are struggling with ADHD, and it doesn't have to be that way! Here is a sensible, low-cost guide for change." *Rachael Bergman, mother of two*

Writers
"Trudy Carlson emerges from pain and loss with a sensible, effective remedy for ADHD children. A must reading for parents and teachers!" *Patt Jackson, Freelance Writer*

Table of Contents

CHAPTER 1 - INTRODUCTION   1

CHAPTER 2 - THE STORY OF BEN'S ADHD   6

    KINDERGARTEN   7
    FIRST GRADE   8
    SECOND GRADE   11
    THIRD GRADE   14
    FOURTH GRADE   16
    FIFTH GRADE   17
    SIXTH GRADE   22
    SEVENTH GRADE   24
    EIGHTH GRADE   26

CHAPTER 3 - THE STORY OF MY DYSLEXIA   27

    MY DYSLEXIA   28
    SEVEN KEY FACTORS   36

CHAPTER 4 - THE BIOLOGY AND TREATMENT OF LEARNING DISABILITIES   42

    THE ANATOMY OF DYSLEXIA   42

THE CHEMISTRY OF ATTENTION DEFICIT	45
WHAT EXPERTS SUGGEST AS EFFECTIVE TREATMENT FOR ADHD	47
Stimulant Medication	48
Parent Training in Contingency Management	50
Self-Control Training	50
Parent-Adolescent Intervention	53
Classroom Management	54
IS ADHD A HANDICAPPING CONDITION?	54
LOW-COST, NO-COST PROGRAMS FOR FAMILIES OF ADHD CHILDREN	56
Support Group	57
Buddy System at School	58
Special After School Sessions	59
Physical Education	60
Cognitive and Interpersonal Skills Training For Older Students	62
Medication and Private Therapy	63

CHAPTER 5 - PORTRAIT OF AN ADHD CHILD   64

SIX BASIC RESEARCH FINDINGS	65
INCONSISTENCIES IN THE BEHAVIOR OF YOUNG PEOPLE WITH ADHD	69
Different Behaviors in Different Settings	69
Situational Variation	74
RULE GOVERNING BEHAVIOR	76
MEDICAL CRITERIA FOR ADHD	78
Ben as an example	82

DEVELOPMENTAL COURSE AND PREDICTORS
OF OUTCOME 85
   Infancy 85
   Preschool 86
   School Age 87

CHAPTER 6 - KIDS HELPING OTHER KIDS — 90

WHY THIS IS AN IMPORTANT SOURCE OF HELP — 91
TEACHING YOUNGSTERS
TO BE PEER TUTORS — 97
SPECIAL CONSIDERATIONS FOR ADHD — 100

CHAPTER 7 - REDUCING STRESS FOR TEACHERS AS WELL AS STUDENTS — 100

TEACHERS DESERVE A BREAK — 100
MY PERSONAL EXPERIENCE AS A TEACHER — 101
THE STORY OF A JUNIOR HIGH TEACHER — 105
SIMPLE ADJUSTMENTS TO SCHOOLS — 107

CHAPTER 8 - IF I RAN A SCHOOL   111

CHAPTER 9 - RESPECTING INDIVIDUAL DIFFERENCES   117
   HISTORICAL PERSPECTIVE   117
   CONTINUED PROBLEMS DESPITE BEST EFFORTS   120
   TYPICAL DISTRIBUTION PATTERNS: SEVERE CASES ARE RARE   122
   AVOIDING LEARNED HELPLESSNESS   124
   ALL LEARNING PROBLEMS NEED TO BE TAKEN SERIOUSLY   126

WORKS CITED   127

FURTHER REFERENCES   128

INDEX   130

ABOUT THE AUTHOR   134

Acknowledgment

No book is the product of just one person. My heartfelt gratitude goes to everyone who contributed to it. I want to thank those individuals who read this work in manuscript form at various stages, including Tracy Pierson, Marj Cox, Ann Sanford, Eileen Gannon, Carol Michealson, Roseann Biever, Margaret Kinetz, Monica Natzel, Carol Nord, Lena Biever, Rod Nord, Rachael Bergman, Lu Harter, Adela Hartman, Jo Stewart, Caroline Carlson, Char Gallian, Dr. Barry Garfinkel, Dr. Elisabeth Kubler-Ross, and Dr. Jerome Kwako.

I would like to make special mention of Kristen Oberg, Patt Jackson, and Robin Blatnik, the editors of the book, whose skill and encouragement helped to make it what it is. Their sustained commitment to this project is the kind of help writers dream of receiving, but never expect to get.

I wish to express appreciation to all the works that are quoted in this book. The list of these is contained in the bibliography.

There can be no full accounting of the debt I owe to the scores of people who contributed to this project by giving me advice and/or technical assistance. They include Dr. Aaron Beck, Dr. Drake Duane, Joseph Gallian, James Perlman, and Sheldon Aubut. Special thanks to my brothers and sisters who helped in a number of ways.

The cover is designd by David Garon, and the painting on the cover is by Garry Carlson

Chapter 1

Introduction

Young people with learning disabilities sometimes commit suicide. One bright young man, previously misdiagnosed as retarded, expressed his sense of hopelessness and helplessness by writing, "If you tell a person he is less than a person long enough, he'll start to believe it. Ever since I started school, and even before, I was told I was less than a person."

Because he had difficulty in English and math, the subjects he felt were important, he thought his status among his peers was low. He believed the label "dumb" and "stupid" applied to him even though he was proficient in science. Discouraged and disheartened, the young man faced what seemed to him to be overwhelming challenges. His concluding remark was, "We live in a society where directly or indirectly we tell people they are less than persons, and we preach that everybody is created equal."

This young man's actual IQ was in the high 130's, placing him in the near-genius category. His learning disability was dyslexia; a difficulty in learning to read, spell and master a foreign language. Persons with dyslexia are three times more likely to suffer from depression than are people without a learning disability. Dyslexia plus depression meant he struggled with two disabilities, not just one.

I, too, have dyslexia. Mine is a mild case, and I was spared the pain of depressive illness, but it has made me sensitive to the problems associated with any learning problem. This book explores not only the story of my dyslexia, but more important to me, my son Ben's struggle with attention deficit hyperactive disorder. Ben suffered from a combination of ADHD, depressive illness, and anxiety disorder. Like the young man who wrote the essay, Ben's co-morbidity (having more than one problem) led him to helplessness and hopelessness. Like the other young man, Ben committed suicide.

I purposely use the death of these two bright young men to make the point that learning disabilities are very serious problems for youngsters. I did not fully appreciate the seriousness of these conditions until Ben's death made the connection between learning problems and destructive behavior all too real.

When I had Ben evaluated through the Mayo Clinic in Rochester, Minnesota, and discovered he had ADHD rather than dyslexia, I mistakenly concluded that an attention deficit was not as serious a problem as a reading disability. My misperception about ADHD was probably shared by many other parents and teachers. Any teacher who does not know the student well may not even realize that the child with ADHD has a problem. I recall a remark one of Ben's seventh grade teachers once made regarding Ben's behavior: "There was absolutely no reason for him to act the way he did." I responded by saying that if Ben's problem was blindness there would be understanding, but Ben's problems were invisible. After my son's death, my initial anger made me wonder if his teacher would now be willing to concede that there actually was something legitimately wrong with Ben.

My son's ADHD and my dyslexia are two very different learning problems. I struggled with my problem during my own childhood, and with Ben's problem during my adulthood. I understood his less because ADHD is more baffling. I made the false assumption that the way I had learned to cope with my problem (increased effort) could also work for him. I should have listened more carefully to his insightful remark, "You are you and I am me. I'm different."

Because I have dyslexia myself, I feel I can speak with genuine understanding of that condition while advocating for fair treatment for young people with ADHD. The study of dyslexia has a rich history. There is a wealth of research on the topic; teachers are generally more aware of the nature of that particular learning disability, and special programs are geared to work with children with reading problems. We are only beginning to understand and properly treat attention deficit hyperactive disorder. Children who have difficulty concentrating, sitting still, following directions, and completing assignments are often thought of as having only motivational problems or poor work habits.

Youngsters with dyslexia are usually seen as having a legitimate learning problem in the specific subjects of reading and spelling. On the other hand, children who have ADHD have problems with attention, impulsivity and overactivity, and are not often seen as having a legitimate learning disability. The illegitimacy of ADHD is underscored by the fact that in many cases the child with attention deficits will not qualify for school services, as would a child with dyslexia. Partly because schools realize they cannot afford to provide expensive programs for the large number of students who have this problem, their only response often has been to recommend medical treatment. This differential response by the school, however, may lead many parents and teachers to falsely assume that ADHD is not as important a problem as dyslexia.

I hope we are now living in a time of inclusion rather than exclusion. The challenge in our age of huge Federal budget deficits is to embrace simple, no cost/low cost programs for youngsters with a wide range of learning and emotional problems. It is essential these programs be applicable and available to all students, relatively easy to implement, and helpful in reducing stress for parents. They should avoid increasing the work load for already overworked teachers, while increasing the comfort level for students who are struggling.

The suggested programs in this book do just that. The emphasis is on cooperation among students, coupled with the option of increased exposure by students to fewer teachers -- all of which can make life easier for everyone involved. It is a simple method which reintroduces into today's classrooms the warmth and reduced stress we enjoyed in the past. What is proposed here is only an option. It need not interfere with the freedom of choice for those parents, teachers, and students who wish to continue with the current system, if it is working well for them. It does, however, provide a welcome alternative to the many young people today who are in need of support.

The suicide rate among young people has tripled in the last three decades. This statistic leads us to ask, "What is going on in society that causes adolescents to give up on life?" And it is not just the suicide rate that is alarming; it is estimated that 10 percent of young people have serious depression and an additional 29 percent have mild to moderate cases of the condition. All youngsters face high levels of stress coming from a wide array of sources. The emotional support provided in a program which encourages cooperation among peers and the use of each other's talents can be helpful to everyone.

Youngsters with learning problems face the challenges of coping with the difficulties of their disabilities along with the high level of stress faced by all students today. Dyslexia is a serious problem for any youngster, especially if depression accompanies it. ADHD is very common, and an equally serious problem for the students who have it; their parents who attempt to help them cope with it, their teachers who work with these youngsters, and the other students in the classroom who are affected by the child's behavior. Taking all learning disabilities seriously and dealing with them by the use of realistic, effective, and inexpensive methods is a fair way of treating everyone who deserves help. As everyone is given options, hopelessness and helplessness may be reduced.

Chapter 2

The Story of Ben's ADHD

When a child commits suicide, parents will often say, "If only I had done this, things might have been different. If only I had done that, I might have prevented the death." We hear experts explain how a particular technique might work effectively to solve a problem; we read of methods that might prevent tragedy. When the unthinkable happens, parents or teachers often assume that an untried method **would** have worked to solve the problem.

This is not always true. What follows is an account of all we did to help our son, Ben, cope with his attention deficit hyperactive disorder (ADHD). The reason for this thorough account is not to prove what conscientious parents we were. Rather it is used to point out that even parents with a background in education and psychology may not be able, by themselves, to prevent a child's death.

Many methods do work very well. As a teacher, I had many successes with other people's children. I also made recommendations to other parents which resulted in significant improvements. But, some students find coping difficult because their particular problems are neither simple nor easy to solve. Ben's story is an example of this. He had a complex depressive condition. Since most people with depression also have an anxiety disorder, this adds to their difficulties. (These two conditions are described in more detail in my book, The Suicide of My Son.) The focus here is Ben's struggle with ADHD, the attempts of his teachers to help him, and my efforts to assist him with school work and to obtain evaluation and treatment for his condition.

KINDERGARTEN

Ben was five and one-half when he started kindergarten. He never was the kind of child who spent time putting together puzzles, coloring, or doing other quiet activities for any length of time. I sent him to nursery school for part of the year preceding kindergarten in the hope of increasing his readiness for school routine.

The emphasis in Ben's kindergarten year was on social adjustment, not academic skills. Because of this, I would often play simple games with Ben to teach him his ABC's. Ben was cooperative and well motivated during this tutoring situation. He seemed to enjoy learning and had an adequate memory. Playing games with him on a one-to-one basis worked well for him at this time. Nothing in these early experiences indicated to me he would have a learning problem.

FIRST GRADE

It was in first grade, as academic work began in earnest, that Ben's problem attending to tasks and getting his work done became apparent. Several weeks after school started, his teacher sent his unfinished work home with a note saying that Ben had a backlog of unfinished work, and perhaps he would feel better about himself if he could catch up and make a fresh start. I appreciated her concern, agreed with her suggestion, and set about helping him.

Left on his own, Ben just sat in front of his work rather than doing it. I thought if I made sure he completed his assignments he would learn three important lessons:

1. *The teacher and I were working as a team.*

2. *His work was going to be done by him. (Although I would give him additional teaching if necessary, I would not supply answers or give unnecessary assistance).*

3. *If he did not work in school he would then miss opportunities to play or watch TV at home.*

With these three reasons for doing his work, I hoped he would see that it made no sense to just sit and do nothing in school. Not understanding the nature of his problem, I believed teaching him the importance of completing work in school would solve everything. I hoped once this original batch of incomplete work was done, Ben would be able to keep up on his own. Of course, I was wrong. ADHD students have an ongoing problem completing assignments in school.

Throughout Ben's school years, I tried a variety of approaches in an attempt to create an environment conducive to completing school assignments. During his first grade year, I had Ben do his work at the kitchen table while I cooked dinner and washed dishes. But he did not seem to be able to focus on his work.

In my attempt to understand and cope with Ben's problem, I wondered if his lack of concentration was manipulative. I was familiar with research indicating that some children learn to behave inappropriately because misbehavior gets attention. I asked myself, "Was Ben using his incomplete work as a means of getting extra help and attention from his teacher and me?" With this in mind, I was careful to give extra attention to Ben only when he was doing what he was supposed to do. In order to reinforce work behavior, I paid attention to Ben when he was working and withdrew my attention when he stopped. I needed to give him positive, but non-interfering, reinforcement while he struggled on his own with his school work.

I decided to sit beside him after I finished my housework and read a book. I wanted to act as a role model of someone quietly focusing on a task. While reading, I would also reinforce Ben. My son, like most people, liked to have his back rubbed; so, as long as his pencil was moving I would rub his back. As soon as his pencil stopped moving, I would stop rubbing his back.

According to learning theory, reinforcement of "on-task" behavior should produce results. Doing work and getting his back rubbed meant that school tasks should ultimately take on pleasant associations, and he would begin to feel good about doing them. Behavior modification theory says his performance should improve. This method of reinforcement did help Ben finish that night's work, but it could not permanently fix his attention deficit.

What I failed to see was that his inability to do his work had nothing to do with his being uncooperative or manipulative. It had everything to do with the neurotransmitters in his brain. I had tried to condition him to develop good work habits. Conditioning is helpful, but conditioning alone is not totally effective against a problem caused by brain chemistry.

Attempts to help Ben get his work done became an ongoing process. Once or twice each week Ben's first grade teacher would send his unfinished work home. I, in turn, helped him attend to the task. I was hopeful Ben would adjust to the expectations of school, and sometime during the next year or so he would develop efficient work habits.

SECOND GRADE

Ben continued to have problems getting his work done. Realizing that Ben had done much of his school work at home the previous year, his second grade teacher wondered if his reliance on working at home had not undermined the importance of doing it independently at school. His teacher wanted Ben to do all his work in the classroom. She developed a program of shortening his assignments to help him accomplish this goal.

Starting with shortened assignments, she hoped to gradually increase the amount of work he would do by himself at school. For example, if Ben could only do three to five problems on a 30-problem worksheet, she would only assign five problems, and would praise him when these were completed. By doing this, she hoped to establish a situation in which Ben would be getting the assigned number of problems done. After succeeding at this level, she would move the criteria up to seven or eight problems. Once this was accomplished, the criteria would be raised to ten problems, and so forth. The strategy was to increase performance slowly, never to expect more than Ben had proved capable of doing, and to reinforce Ben's efforts. The whole system was logical and positive. Like me, she hoped there was a way to teach him a lesson that would permanently develop a habit of getting his work done independently at school.

Shortening the length of assignments is one recommended treatment strategy for working with children with attention deficits. Like the conditioning I had used at home, it is a helpful tool, but alone it cannot create miracles for a child with ADHD.

My point is this: Ben's first grade teacher was fantastic. Her methods were appropriate. She did not fail him. Likewise, Ben's second grade teacher was wonderful. Her teaching was excellent, her motivation high. She, too, did not fail him. But Ben had a genetically-based biological illness which prevailed over all our efforts. If either of those teachers would have had Ben for two years rather than just one, their chance of finding a method that would have been more effective would have increased. Pairing him up with a buddy/tutor also would have helped him.

During Ben's second grade, my own efforts to understand him led me to make several observations. Ben was still reversing many of the letters he printed. Although reversals are fairly common in first grade, they typically begin to disappear during the second year. Ben's were not disappearing. This should have been a helpful indicator that something organic was wrong. Ben's written work was hard to read, unorganized, messy. We as parents and teachers often have difficulty interpreting what we see. Sloppy work gives the impression that the student is doing it too quickly or does not care about doing a good job. But for many students, handwriting is often a visual indicator of a learning disability.

Not only did I fail to fully understand what I saw, but I did not understand what I heard. Ben's jumbled speech (consisting of sentences in which the words were out of order) was also a clue to the organic nature of his problem.

As second grade came to an end, I was perplexed. Ben's teacher had shortened all of his assignments, which meant he had not done the full amount of work for second grade. I wondered if Ben should do some academic work during the summer to help prepare him for third grade. Doing a little school work during the summer would at least help him retain what he had already learned.

Ben was still adding and subtracting with his fingers. I hoped rote practice on addition and subtraction would give him mastery of simple calculation before he was asked to tackle multiplication and division in third grade. I copied one sheet of addition problems and a separate sheet of subtraction problems. I had him do the same work sheets day after day because I thought he would develop more self-confidence from truly mastering this one task. I hoped he would feel more comfortable with math knowing there was at least one thing he could do well.

I also wanted him to do some daily reading. Reading at bedtime, rather than during the day, meant it would not interfere with his opportunity to play. Although he was not motivated to read, he agreed to try. It was our custom to take turns reading -- I would read one page, and he would read the next one as we went through the story. My reading every other page was beneficial for a number of reasons: Ben was able to read a whole story without tiring. (Frequent breaks **are** a recommended procedure for kids with ADHD). Breaks not only gave him an opportunity to rest and listen, but also allowed him to understand the story better. Hearing every other page read with proper intonation, he was able to comprehend some parts of the story as it unfolded. We also stopped several times during the story and spent time discussing what was happening to the characters. This gave him not only another break in his reading, but also some work on comprehension. This method of reading did work well for us and we both enjoyed it.

THIRD GRADE

When Ben went to third grade, he was expected to do a full work load, but was allowed to bring his unfinished work home each evening. Rather than doing work at the kitchen table as he had done in the past, we set up a desk for him in his room so he would have a quiet environment, free of distraction. I sent him to his room to do his work and would check on him often. I found he got little work done on his own.

Ben, like many ADHD students, needed lots of support. Without someone close at hand, he could not complete much work. Left on his own, he just could not function. He must have felt lonely sitting at his desk, unable to do his work while I was busy in the kitchen. Unfinished work kept him away from the rest of the family and prevented him from being able to do anything he might have enjoyed. I felt sorry for him.

After I was finished with my housework I would join him in his room, bringing a book of my own to read while he did his school work. To help him get started, I would review the examples in his textbook to make sure he understood how he was to do the assignment. After one assignment was done, we would tackle the next subject until each one was finished.

The need to help Ben complete unfinished school work meant I was chained to Ben's homework for two to four hours each evening, Monday through Thursday. Consequently, each day I would get up, go to work, come home, make dinner, clean house, supervise Ben's home work for several hours, then drop exhausted into bed. I repeated this each week from September to June. Does that sound like fun? Well, it was not any fun for Ben either. He sat in front of uncompleted school work rather than being involved in activities that might have brought some joy into his life.

Schoolwork is important and necessary. Research clearly indicates that the more time children spend on school work, the better they are at it. If we want our children to be competent in math and reading, it is vitally important that they spend a significant amount of time in their childhood doing academic work. However, for children with an attention deficit disorder and depression, schoolwork can be a nightmare for them and their parents.

To put some fun into learning, I purchased the educational electronic device, "Speak and Spell," a small hand held talking computer with separate cartridges which teaches words at different grade levels. When Ben showed some enthusiasm for it, I also purchased the "Speak and Read" and "Speak and Math." I hoped these electronic tutors would do better than I could in helping Ben with the basics. These devices never run out of patience, never are too busy to be available, and unless the batteries wear out, they never run out of energy. Ben used them a lot in the years which followed, especially when he was home from school because of illness. He also used them at bedtime when he was not feeling sleepy. I do not know how much they were able to help him with his academic skills, but they held his attention for a time.

When summer came at the end of third grade, I again had Ben do a little school work. This time I used a number of different math work sheets and he did a little nighttime reading. I also encouraged Ben to use the speaking computers on his own.

FOURTH GRADE

As fourth grade began, I helped Ben every evening by supervising his homework and often teaching him. It was the only way he had to get some idea of how to do the work. But I was getting worn out with the nightly homework routine. In Ben's first years of elementary school, I still had hope that his work pattern would change. By fourth grade, with no improvement in sight, I became increasingly concerned. The research I remembered indicated that if children do not take responsibility for doing well in school by sixth grade, it is not likely they will ever do so. I had already spent several years supervising and helping Ben with his homework. I did not honestly feel I had the energy to continue this through upper elementary, junior high, and high school. I believed Ben had a learning disability. I wanted him to get services through the school so he could do some work there. I requested an evaluation by the learning disabilities (L.D.) teacher.

Ben's evaluation was done in October of fourth grade. He was given a battery of tests that measured both aptitude (ability) and achievement. (The results of this testing are more fully described in Chapter 5 under the heading

"Different Behaviors in Different Settings.") Ben's score on this individually-administered test indicated his deficit was not significant enough for him to qualify for learning disabilities help. But like most students with ADHD, his performance in one setting was very different from his performance in another. As you will read in further chapters, Ben's score on that individually-given battery of tests was vastly different from his score on the group-administered achievement test done in his classroom that same year.

With no help from school forthcoming, I looked into the possibility of getting someone other than myself to help him with his homework. I knew a former teacher who was willing to tutor Ben each day after school for a couple of months. Later, when the teacher was unable to continue, I hired a thirteen-year-old friend of my daughter to take over the tutoring during the last few months of the year.

FIFTH GRADE

Entering his upper elementary years meant that Ben had two teachers rather than just one. Ben liked both of his new teachers very much and wanted to perform well for them, but his difficulty in getting his work done legibly and on time continued nonetheless. It was then I did some investigating about learning disabilities on my own. A pamphlet distributed at the meeting of our local association of parents of children with learning disabilities says:

What are the Symptoms of a Learning Disability?

Learning disabilities aren't always easy to spot. That's why they are called a "hidden" handicap. In addition, the kinds of problems and the severity of the problems are very different for different people. Each learning disabled child/adult shows a unique combination of problems.

However, some of the signs that may indicate a learning disability are:

- short attention span (restless, easily distracted)

- reverses letters and numbers (sees `b' for `d', `6' for `9')

- reads poorly, if at all (below age and grade level)

- often confused about direction and time (right-left, up-down, yesterday-tomorrow)

- personal disorganization (can't follow simple schedules)

- impulsive and inappropriate behavior (poor judgment in social situations, talks and acts before thinking)

- poor coordination (clumsy, has trouble using pencil, scissors, crayons)

- inconsistent performance (can't remember today what was learned yesterday)

- fails written tests but scores high on oral exams (or vice versa)

- speech problems (immature speech development, has trouble expressing ideas)

Some of these problems can be found in all children at certain stages of development. But, if a child has a cluster of these symptoms, which do not disappear as he/she gets older, you might suspect a learning disability. (Author unknown)

This described Ben. He was always disorganized about his work, no matter how great the organizational folder we bought for him each September. Unfortunately, he would often end up re-doing assignments because he did not have the slightest idea where in his messy desk to find his already half-finished work. Besides disorganization, inability to concentrate was a major factor. The reason he had difficulty getting started with his work was that he did not understand what he was expected to do. Any teacher who did not understand his problem would assume Ben had not been listening. He may have been listening, but with his attention deficit, he was unable to follow what was said. With his inability to concentrate, Ben was not able to work on the task.

I attended a conference on learning disabilities in April of 1985. The keynote speaker, Dr. Drake Duane, a neurologist from the Mayo Clinic in Rochester, Minnesota, spoke on the topic, "The Learning Brain: Neurology of Exceptionality." His speech centered on recent scientific discoveries of the anatomy and biology of the brain. He said that scientists could now prove what good special education teachers have always contended: namely, that persons with learning disabilities do have valuable strengths and talents that should be emphasized and developed. This implies that teachers and parents should accentuate the things students do well, and, when possible, de-emphasize or not expect the person to work on tasks students find especially difficult. I kept this in mind when thinking about ways to help Ben.

For example, Ben showed talent for using a computer. Using it would emphasize his strengths and it could help him in a number of different ways. He could type his work rather than go through the laborious process of writing. We hoped it would make his school work a little more enjoyable. He could also use a spelling program to find his errors and correct them. Because Ben's handwriting was poor, we thought his teachers might be relieved to get typed assignments rather than his usual messy papers. For this child with an attention deficit, we hoped working at the computer might hold his attention better than doing handwritten work. In summer, we purchased the computer and Ben went to summer school to learn keyboarding.

The neurologist who spoke at the conference on learning disabilities also gave a second lecture entitled "Attention Deficit Disorder: Characteristics, Implication and Treatment." In this lecture, he gave a review of current medical approaches to treatment. He mentioned that a small dose of antidepressant medication is often helpful to patients with ADHD. A few weeks after the conference I took Ben to a local psychiatrist for an evaluation regarding the possible use of the medication. That doctor was not willing to prescribe it.

In my efforts to seek help, I also discovered a private agency in our town which provided tutors for children with learning disabilities. At the conference at the end of Ben's fifth grade year, I mentioned to the teachers that Ben was scheduled to be re-evaluated and would likely receive services from a specialized tutor from that private agency. I also requested that Ben be re-evaluated for learning disability services from the school system.

Ben was again evaluated by the LD teacher from the school system in May of 1986. At the end of the month we met to review the findings. The same individualized test was administered and the results were similar to the earlier test. (Ben's scores were again much higher on the individually administered test than his scores on the group-administered test done in the classroom.)

In my frustration the spring of Ben's fifth grade year, it occurred to me to take Ben to the Mayo Clinic for an evaluation. The question still remained in my mind: was Ben's problem just a matter of work habits and motivation, or did he in fact have a learning disability? If we could not get a definitive answer to the question at the Mayo Clinic, we probably could not get an answer any place else either. I wrote and was given an appointment for him in September.

In the meantime, Ben was evaluated by a private learning center, and the specialized tutoring they recommended was begun. It focused on training in reading and writing. This was certainly helpful to him, but of course this could not help him with his core problem: an attention deficit.

SIXTH GRADE

Ben had his appointment at the Mayo Clinic soon after sixth grade began. At the end of the three-day evaluation, I attended the summary conference where the results of all the testing were presented. The team's recommendations were made at this time. There were three significant observations: First, Ben's verbal IQ was at the 77th percentile, while his performance IQ was at the 37th percentile. Verbally he was above average, but he performed markedly below average. Second, Ben had a noticeable emotional dysfunctioning. Third, he had a mild but significant difficulty with attention.

The team recommended that Ben

- begin an antidepressant medication for the attention control impairment,

- be considered for LD services at school in the areas of spelling and written language,

- see a psychiatrist on an outpatient basis for at least a trial period.

When the November teachers' conferences were scheduled, we wrote a note to the school letting his teachers know we would share the Mayo Clinic report with them. His homeroom teacher met with us initially. Later, we had a second meeting with the principal and both of his teachers. His other teacher had objected to Ben doing his work on the computer. She felt using the computer would interfere with working to improve his handwriting. The principal supported Ben's use of the computer. The principal also mentioned that although Ben had been denied services by the LD teacher on two previous occasions, we could request a conciliation conference to further discuss the issue.

From this experience I learned that if you can persevere, even the most impenetrable system may ultimately see the logic behind your requests. Although we did not get LD services for our son, we did get better cooperation from the school administration and from the teacher who originally objected to the use of the computer.

The remaining time in sixth grade seemed to go smoothly. Ben spent time studying for his social studies and science tests with his father, and he did well. He was doing some of his English and spelling assignments on the computer. He was going to his tutor regularly.

The last conference in elementary school was devoted to the subject of planning for junior high. Ben's homeroom teacher gave us a helpful piece of advice that is important for students with learning disabilities. Ben had expressed interest in signing up for band. I was not sure it was a good idea. I had heard horror stories from other parents about the difficulty they had getting their children to practice. We certainly did not need any added problems getting Ben to do assignments at home. He needed help with everything he did, and I could not imagine helping him with a band instrument. I neither played an instrument nor had I learned to read music. I did not have any idea where he would get help if he needed it. Some of the brightest students in junior high signed up for band, including students who had previous musical training such as piano lessons. I feared Ben would be in over his head.

Ben's teacher disagreed. In a very straightforward way he acted as an advocate for Ben, asking me to give him a chance at exploring something new. He said, "Who knows? It might be something he would be good at." This made me think twice. Ben really wanted to try, so I let him. I will always be glad I did. Band would turn out to be a place Ben excelled -- something every student with a learning problem desperately needs.

SEVENTH GRADE

I was concerned that two of the core symptoms of ADHD (inability to concentrate and impulsivity) would prove especially challenging for Ben during junior high. Disorganization and problems getting assignments completed would be difficult as Ben changed teachers and classrooms each hour. (My numerous concerns about the junior high school setting and his experiences there are more fully described in my book The Suicide of My Son.)

The summer before seventh grade, Ben's tutor discovered that her careful instruction focused on reading and spelling skills was not solving Ben's major learning problems. Subsequently, she suggested we discontinue her services. Ben and I spent the summer using the computer to type the three research papers I knew would be assigned in his upcoming health class. Having these important assignments already completed, I hoped, would help him feel more prepared for school when it started in September.

Seventh grade progressed better than expected. Ben loved band and was good at it. He and his band teacher became friends. Disorganized Ben was particularly helped by the structure provided by his highly organized math teacher. Ben was interested in health, and the already completed research papers meant he did well in that class. Because half of his work load consisted of classes Ben found manageable, his life went better in seventh grade than I had expected, and his grades were fine.

At the end of the school year I became less concerned about his problems with concentration, but more concerned about the impulsivity symptom of the disorder. When summer came around, I focused on keeping him busy and out of trouble. Ben did manual work rather than academics. We also started the long process of getting treatment for his depression from an adolescent psychiatrist who was highly competent in treating mood disorders.

EIGHTH GRADE

Ben had no real academic support during eighth grade. He was not getting private tutoring anymore; he did not have the advantage of having some assignments already completed as he had when he started seventh grade, and his new math teacher did not provide the highly structured system Ben found so helpful the previous year. I thought the medications prescribed by his psychiatrist for depression would improve his ability to concentrate to the point that he could manage on his own. I was mistaken.

Problems completing work persisted for Ben, as they do with other young people with ADHD who need structure and support on a daily basis. During the year, Ben had some incompletes on his report card. I had no way of knowing what assignments were due each day. Ben did not provide that information, either because he did not know himself or because he was so discouraged about school that he just wanted to avoid doing the work.

The one bright spot in his life was band. He loved his trombone, and spent extra time with his teacher. Finding one subject in which students with ADHD can shine can do a lot to help kids who are struggling, but that is not the only solution. They need support in the classes they find overwhelming.

At the end of May, all assignments for the semester were due. At the end of May, Ben also had an experimental reduction in his medication. On May 31, 1989, Ben shot himself.

Chapter 3

The Story of My Dyslexia

Not everyone who has a learning disability is doomed. Fortunately, many people with difficulties overcome them. The question is, why do some people with a disability learn to cope with it, while others continue to be plagued by it? Researchers and educators began to unravel the mystery by studying dyslexia. As I mentioned earlier, I have some understanding of children and adults with this condition because I have dyslexia myself. There is no better way for me to demonstrate the differences between one type of learning disability, dyslexia, and another type of learning problem, attention deficit hyperactive disorder, than by briefly telling the story of my years in elementary school.

My purpose in doing so is threefold. First, since dyslexia was the first learning disability to be thoroughly investigated, it is the most widely understood of the LD's (learning disabilities) and is accepted as a legitimate cause of learning problems. In some states, the laws funding LD programs in schools are heavily weighted towards dyslexia. Dyslexic youngsters often qualify for special services from the school, while parents of youngsters with attention deficits are told their children do not have a genuine learning problem, but are just "unmotivated."

The second purpose in telling my story is to point out what I could do to help myself because I luckily had only one problem -- a mild case of dyslexia. This contrasts dramatically with Ben, who faced multiple conditions: his attention deficit hyperactive disorder, a complex depressive condition, and an anxiety disorder. Children like Ben can not just "work harder and pull themselves up by their boot straps."

Finally, I was fortunate in my school career and was ultimately successful. My story illustrates seven key factors that students with learning disabilities need to help them cope. I did not have any specialized services to help me, but our school was able to use some simple, no-cost methods that were helpful. It is precisely these no-cost or low-cost methods which are important in today's era of budget restraints. In the chapters ahead, I will be outlining ways to help children with ADHD, as well as other youngsters who need extra help and support. When children feel they are understood and supported in their efforts, they are then given hope for the future.

MY DYSLEXIA

Dyslexia is a Greek word meaning "word blindness." Although I had normal intelligence, I had a great deal of difficulty learning to read. In first grade, I realized that other students were not having trouble learning new words, but I could not figure them out. I tried lots of strategies to cope.

Sounding out the word letter by letter sometimes helped, but it was not always a predictable method. Consonants were fairly predictable, although there were letters like "g" which had one sound in a word like "give" and a very different sound in a word like "giraffe." Vowels were especially unpredictable -- changing their pronunciation with each word.

I sometimes tried to cope with this word blindness by relying on how the word looked. Remembering all the words I had been taught, I would look at the word and guess which one it was. I based most of my guesses on the first letters of the words and how long the word was. However, confronting words like "them," "that," "they," and "then" is hopeless. Words like "saw" and "was" looked exactly the same to me. Neither sounding out words nor guessing worked. I was having trouble reading. I knew it, and when I read out loud everyone else did too. I wanted to do better, but I did not know how. Once I tried a third way of coping that turned out to be a disaster.

One particular Friday our first grade reading class was cut short. Instead of finishing the whole story, we stopped right before it was my turn. The rhythm of our reading class was predictable, and I knew the following Monday our teacher would start exactly where she left off, and I would be asked to read the next page. For the first time I knew exactly which page of the story I would read out loud. I took my book home and read the page over and over again until I knew it perfectly.

When I went to school on Monday I felt confident for the first time about reading out loud. When our teacher called the reading group, I was excited about the prospect of finally reading flawlessly. The teacher called on me to read the page. Everything seemed to be working out exactly as I had hoped. This was my big moment. I would finally be able to read without error or hesitation in front of the class.

I read the page perfectly, but in the kind of sing-song voice characteristic of someone who had practically memorized the page rather than someone who was reading it for the first time. Feeling proud of my performance, I did not expect my teacher's reaction. She told the class that what I had done was not reading but memorizing, something she did not want. I felt humiliated. The impression I got from her, and the one she probably gave to the rest of the class, was that I had done some sort of cheating. Her message was clear. My latest way of trying to cope with my learning disability was not acceptable and was not to be tried again.

Although my reading was not progressing well in first grade, my written work was all right. The word blindness did not impair my ability to concentrate. Every time a student got 100% on a work sheet, the teacher would stamp a star on their paper, as well as on a small card the child kept. Both the child and the teacher used this as a record of the total number of perfect papers for the year. All the children knew how they were doing, and also knew how the others were doing in comparison. At the end of the year there was a prize for the child in each grade who had the most "star papers."

The last week of first grade my teacher told me I was the winner of the prize. This surprised me. I tried to tell her my friend Jackie had more stars than I did. I explained to her how we had figured it out and our calculations matched. The teacher did not listen to me. I do not know if Jackie and I had both miscalculated or if our teacher did not appreciate being corrected by a six-year-old, but there was no changing her mind, and I got the prize.

During second grade our classroom got a new teacher. I remember her as a very kind person, and it was my good fortune she emphasized phonics while teaching reading. When letters have the same pronunciation from word to word, sounding out letters becomes a successful way to read rather than guessing. A child can begin to develop some hope of being able to cope.

My second grade teacher recognized my struggle with reading and assigned me to the first grade reading group. I was not the only second grader to read with the first graders. The other child was a new girl in our class. I will call her Lonnie. She was new to our town, and none of us was familiar with her. Our teacher allowed her to do things the rest of us were not allowed to do. Lonnie brought her doll to school and sometimes sucked her thumb while sitting at her desk. The teacher did not have her do all the seat work the rest of us had to do. We thought there must be some reason our teacher allowed Lonnie to get away with such immature behavior, but we did not know what it was. Years later it would dawn on me that Lonnie may have been mentally retarded. As an adult, I saw other children with Down's

Syndrome, and recognized them as looking very much like her.

I did not mind that I was a second grader reading with the first graders because I was reading at my level. I remember feeling comfortable with a task that fit my level of ability. I do not remember if I read with the second graders when I was in third grade or not, but I distinctly remember failing the reading test at the end of third grade. As a student in a parochial school in the 1950's, I took a battery of achievement tests at the end of each year. I do not know the exact purpose of this testing, but it gave some measure of how we were doing in each subject.

I specifically recall receiving a score of 65% in reading achievement at the end of third grade: a failing score. I felt badly about my performance but my teacher, a very sensitive and kind woman, was quick to point out that I had tried my very best; I had come very close to passing, it was not my fault, and reading was just hard for me. The distinct impression I got was that I was not a "bad" person just because I had difficulty learning to read -- a very important piece of information for a child with a learning problem. When the term "good student" is used to describe someone who does well, students who do not do well may assume that the word "bad" applies to them.

Not only is translating the printed word into an oral sound a mystery to those with dyslexia; equally mystifying is the process of changing the spoken word into its printed form. Dyslexic students have a weakness in both reading and spelling. Therefore, I not only was failing reading, but I would likely fail at spelling as soon as it was added to my curriculum. At our school, failure in two subjects meant repeating the grade. My parents were not fussy about good grades; an A, B, or C were all the same to them. My mother always said, "I do not care how you do in school as long as you try not to fail a grade." We all did what we could to avoid failing two subjects.

Faced with my problems with both reading and spelling, the choice was obvious. Fixing my reading would be far too complicated for my mother to tackle, but helping me pass my weekly spelling test was manageable. Her way of helping me with my spelling consisted of having me study the words each Sunday afternoon and then test me on the words. I hated our Sunday afternoon ritual, but I did pass spelling, and I managed to pass from grade to grade each year.

I had a different teacher for fourth and fifth grades. She continued the emphasis on oral reading, not only in reading class itself, but in a number of other classes as well. For example, social studies was mostly a matter of taking our turn reading out loud from the text. My reading was very halting. If I could not figure out a word, the teacher would tell me what it was. I was often still guessing at words, and when I was wrong the other students would laugh at me. Realizing I would probably be ridiculed, my anxiety level rose before reading, which probably increased the likelihood of errors.

Although reading was a problem, I continued to do well in other subjects where memory of facts or rules was required and in subjects that were logical. Therefore, math was fine, and even social studies work sheets or tests went well. A subject like language arts was manageable because this was a matter of learning grammatical rules and following them. My other asset in school was that I got along with the other children on the playground. As the youngest of nine children, I knew how to get along with others, especially children who were older than me. I felt comfortable on the playground; I fit in.

By the time I was in the sixth, seventh, and eighth grades, things were going fairly well for me. I still was a very weak reader, but I learned that if I studied hard I could manage to do all right. Unlike my son Ben, I was not depressed. Blessed with an especially high energy level, I could use this energy to tackle school work and take this same energy onto the playground, using it in athletic performance which earned the respect of my peers. My high energy level and enthusiasm for games probably translated to "Trudy is an asset on a team." We played baseball on the playground each spring and fall. We took turns being captain and each day we would choose sides. Thanks to my older brother, my batting and catching skills were pretty good, so I was one of the first picked during this daily ritual.

Another situation which helped my self-esteem was the citizenship club which met during school hours every Friday afternoon. The purpose of this club was to teach citizenship by giving us some practical experience in the democratic process. It also encouraged us to act maturely and responsibly. Officers were elected from the eighth grade class, and in my last year of elementary school I became president. Since the focus of the club was to encourage leadership skills and a sense of self-responsibility, there were times when the president of the class would actually run the classroom. It was part of the tradition at our three-room school that the eighth grader who was the recognized leader of the class would take over in the teacher's absence. So when the teacher was called out of the room, I would teach in her absence. This usually meant I would teach for only 10 or 15 minutes, but I distinctly remember the day the furnace acted up and the teacher was gone for several hours. During her absence I taught the 40 - 45 students in our sixth, seventh and eighth grade classroom, and the students continued on with their work routine as if the teacher were there. This says more for the skill of the teacher than it does about me, but it did, nonetheless, boost my self-esteem.

At the end of eighth grade there was special recognition for the students who received the highest scores on the Diocesan achievement tests. A pin was given to the girl and boy with the highest scores. One of the other girls in my class was going to give me some very stiff competition for the prize. I was worried about subjects like spelling and reading, but I figured I could beat her in the other subjects if I studied hard. When the test scores were averaged, I managed to win by the skin of my teeth. Adding to my happiness was the fact that my brother, who had repeated second grade and was in my class from then on, won the prize for the boys.

Isn't it a paradox? At the end of eighth grade, even with my learning disability, I had managed to cope fairly well with school. I was joyful. At the end of his eighth grade, my son Ben committed suicide. What was the difference between Ben's school problems and my own?

SEVEN KEY FACTORS

1. Emphasis on hope.

Suicidal people feel hopeless about the future and helpless to solve their problems. Some theorists think the one thing all suicidal people have in common is some type of problem they perceive as insolvable. The problem could be a serious and incurable illness, a painfully difficult life situation such as an abusive family, or a serious financial problem. Whatever the cause of their problem, when they find themselves in a difficult situation they feel they can neither cope with nor escape from, they may develop a sense of helplessness and hopelessness.

During my first grade year, I was in a situation like this with reading. Fortunately, starting with second grade, phonics training allowed me to feel less helpless. Having a method that worked effectively for my problem and successes in other academic areas prevented me from developing a sense of hopelessness as a student.

2. Dyslexia is a specific problem, limited to difficulties only with reading, spelling, and learning a foreign language. ADHD is a general problem with concentration.

Failure at reading meant humiliation in front of my peers each time I read aloud, but in other classroom work I was as capable as anyone else. My self-concept was not limited to my performance as a reader. My self-esteem also benefited from the stars I received from handing in acceptable papers. In contrast, Ben's ADHD was an inability to concentrate and perform in all subjects. ADHD students are disorganized. They frequently do not complete assignments, or if they manage to do work, it usually looks sloppy and contains errors. Ben's messy desk was filled with half-finished work. The blackboard list of students with unfinished work always included his name. I do not know how often Ben and I struggled at home to do assignments that were half completed in his desk at school. Ben's general difficulty in concentrating meant he could not balance strong performance in some subjects against weak performance in others as I was able to do.

3. I was given tasks which matched my skill level.

When my mentally retarded classmate and I went to read with the first graders, I was not humiliated. I was just being allowed to read at my level. Neither of us were labeled as different; we were simply given work that fit our needs.

As Ben got older, the gap between what he could do and what other students his age could do widened. His normal or high intelligence meant he was fully and painfully aware of his deficit. But because the nature of his disability was not fully recognized by others, he was not given tasks that matched his ability to concentrate.

4. A distinction was made between having a difficulty with reading and being a bad person.

Many sensitive teachers provide emotional support to students who are having difficulty. When I felt badly about my failing marks at the end of third grade, my teacher gave me some support. The clear memory I have now, forty years later, of exactly what she said, demonstrates the long-lasting effect a simple kindness can have. Our conversation may have lasted only a few minutes, but in another sense it lasted a lifetime.

Is there any way for ADHD youngsters like Ben to feel that they are not bad students? I felt my teacher understood my problem, showed me compassion, and provided me with a method of working with it -- phonics training. Ben needed to hear that the school understood his problem and was willing to help by giving him methods of working with it. Ideas to help ADHD youngsters are presented in more detail in upcoming chapters. They consist of little things like taking a full sheet of math problems and cutting it into two or three sections. After each part is done, the child can put it into a "finished work" pocket hanging in front of his desk and take a break. This dramatically increases the number of completed assignments and helps him to organize his work. The amount of work which needs to be redone will be reduced. Dividing up the work makes it more manageable.

The answer for ADHD students and many other young people with problems also lies in letting students help each other. This helps youngsters feel good about themselves rather than bad. What they need is support.

5. The importance of not having everything in your life be a disaster.

As a child I was not just a student, I was also a productive member of my farm family. My poor reading and spelling skills were totally irrelevant to the work I did in the field, in the garden, in the house, and in the barn. As an energetic youngster, I was an asset to my family. How many young people today feel like an asset? My worth as a person was not determined by how I looked or how well I performed in school. My value to my family consisted of how cooperative I was in helping with the family business. My parents were loving people and our relationship was warm, but there was also something wonderfully objective about knowing I was of tangible value to them.

Do young people with ADHD see themselves as a liability rather than an asset? They need reassurance and emotional support, but they also benefit from opportunities to be of tangible benefit to others. To balance our focus on how to help them, perhaps we could also focus on how they can help us and each other. We do not misuse children by allowing them to do productive work. Wouldn't we all feel more positive towards these difficult students if they were the ones who did community service work like raking and mowing lawns, or shoveling snow for the elderly or the sick? If we set our minds to finding ways these active young people could ease the burdens of others, we may come up with lots of productive things for them to do. I will never forget when Ben said that the best day he ever had in junior high was the day he helped fold and stack chairs in the auditorium. Allowing youngsters to see themselves as helpers rather than as a nuisance is the essence of any work on self-esteem. Low self-esteem is common among students with a variety of emotional problems, not just ADHD. It is an important ingredient for all people who need help and support.

6. *Having one area in which you shine.*

I will not bore you with any of my stories as a first baseman or as a pitcher, but can you imagine what it means to a child with a learning disability to know that every day at recess and at noon hour, she would get to show off what she did best? I was lucky. Unfortunately, all during the six years of elementary school my son Ben never had anything in which he shone. Having frequent validation of our worth among our peers is an essential experience for a child with a learning disability. Knowing others see us as good at something helps to balance those memories of being laughed at when we do poorly in something else, like reading.

Team sports, which involve complex rules, taking your turn, and periods of relative inactivity, are difficult and frustrating for students with ADHD. My attempts to involve Ben in baseball and other group sports were disappointing for me and painful for Ben; but like most students with ADHD, individual sports worked well for him. Ben was a great swimmer, he benefited from martial arts training, and he loved everything he did with horses. Joining the band was one of the best things that ever happened to him. Playing the trombone in junior high was something in which he could shine. Most ADHD students can shine at something. Finding it, and having others see it, is part of that which will sustain them during their frustrations.

7. Developing social skills is important.

My dyslexia did not produce any disability in social skills. I was also fortunate in having a club at school which allowed me to develop some leadership skills. ADHD youngsters are not going to receive any positive feedback from peers unless they receive training in basic social skills. Many of the impulsive things they do (inability to wait their turn or follow the rules of the game, making inconsiderate remarks, or using inappropriate ways of getting attention) cause their peers to avoid playing with them. These impulsive students may also be aggressive, causing even greater rejection. ADHD students need social skills training of some kind in elementary school. It could be organized much like any other club which raises social consciousness, or gives opportunities to practice social skills in recreational activities (Chapter 4).

ADHD students need supportive training in junior and senior high school. (The proposed class "Personal logic and interpersonal skills training, "with wide applicability for any student who needs emotional support, is described in the chapter "What's To Be Done," in The Suicide of My Son.)

What was the difference between my school experience and Ben's? In a nutshell: I found a way to cope; Ben did not. I had only one problem; Ben had three. My problem was confined to the limited spheres of reading and spelling; Ben's problems affected every aspect of his life. I was not overwhelmed. Ben was.

Chapter 4

The Biology and Treatment of Learning Disabilities

A person with dyslexia and depression may commit suicide just like a person with ADHD and depression. It is the presence of two conditions that makes adolescents especially at risk for suicide. I am emphasizing ADHD because it has not been understood in the past. Even though it is common in children, it often goes untreated. It is worth asking the following question relative to both dyslexia and ADHD: Are these learning problems actually physical problems? Those of us who struggle with problems that appear to be a matter of personal weakness and/or a behavioral disorder need to know that these are matters of anatomy and chemistry, not moral fiber.

THE ANATOMY OF DYSLEXIA

My word blindness (dyslexia) related to the anatomy of the back portion of the left side of my brain, the part largely responsible for speech. Dyslexics have difficulty with reading and spelling because of the anatomy of that part of the brain, the speech center. Many people with dyslexia have delayed speech as young children and have great difficulty learning a foreign language in high school or college. If they only have dyslexia, their ability to concentrate is not impaired and they can do well in other subjects.

Our brains consist of two halves: the left hemisphere and the right hemisphere. The left hemisphere of the brain does the talking, reading, spelling, and learning of foreign languages. The left hemisphere is typically larger than the right. Nearly 65 percent of the population have a brain whose left side is larger and subsequently well-equipped to enable them to read, to spell, and to do other speech related skills. About 25 percent of the population have a brain whose hemispheres are equal in size. This leaves approximately 10 percent of the population whose right side of the brain is larger than the left. Autopsy studies of dyslexics were conducted by Harvard neurologist Dr. Albert Galaburda and his co-workers in 1989. The autopsied brains of ten persons with dyslexia revealed that a wedge-shaped region of the temporal lobe were equal in size. But there is more to the story of the anatomy of dyslexia. The brain of the dyslexic is characterized by three other factors.

First, the brain is not only organized left and right, but front to back, as well as top to bottom. Certain types of cells are typically found in specific locations, but brain cells can migrate from one location to another. During the development of the fetus, some of the brain cells typically move to a new location. Researchers find that in the brain of dyslexics there are clumps of nerve cells left behind in a region from which they should have migrated.

Second, the brain of the dyslexic is also characterized by faulty organization. The term used to describe this is dysplasia. Researchers describe the organization of neurons in the brain of a dyslexic as being "in minor disarray" (Duane, 1991).

Third, the surface of the brain is made of gray tissue. An infant's brain is only slightly wrinkled, but as the person grows older, the wrinkles get deeper. A fully grown adult has a brain weighing about three pounds. Although multiple folds and curves are typical for everyone, autopsy studies of persons with dyslexia reveal the existence of "many microscopic in-foldings of the brain trapped beneath the cortical surface." (Duane, 1991) In other words, the dyslexic has a number of small folds below the outer part of his or her brain that are not typically found in the brain of a person who does not have dyslexia.

These three characteristics are found in both hemispheres of the brain but are more prevalent in the left side. They are especially prevalent along the Sylvian fissure, the portion of the brain especially important to language function. All of this evidence leads to the conclusion that "word blindness" is a problem of brain anatomy.

The dyslexic does not usually have low intelligence. Instead, dyslexia is simply a condition in which the brain's left hemisphere is smaller than the right and has unusual cell organization. Although scientists have several interesting theories about why this condition develops, no single theory has yet been established as generally accepted fact. One causal theory looked at the level of testosterone present during the first trimester of the baby's development in utero, the time when the right side of the brain is developing rapidly. A second theory focused at the working of the mother's immune system during the development of the fetus.

In October of 1994 scientists published the results of a study which examined three generations of families with reading disorders, and found a genetic basis for dyslexia. Researchers at four institutions combined data from two groups of reading disabled people, including sets of fraternal twins, to trace the reading problems to a gene located somewhere in chromosome number six.

Dyslexia had been thought to be three-and-one-half times more common in males than in females. However, there is some current research which seriously questions this. Previous figures showed that dyslexia affected approximately 6 percent of the population, but since more girls are now being diagnosed as dyslexic, the percentage of the population with this disorder may be larger than originally suspected.

THE CHEMISTRY OF ATTENTION DEFICIT

Whereas dyslexia is a condition resulting from brain anatomy, attention deficit hyperactive disorder may be a result of brain chemistry. Specifically, it is a problem of the neurotransmitters, as they affect particular areas of the brain. In ADHD: A Guide to Understanding and Helping Children with Attention Deficit Hyperactivity Disorder in School Settings, Braswell and her colleagues write,

Current research is focusing on the frontal and prefrontal regions of the brain which are involved in both the regulation of attention and the inhibition of sensory information. Using recently developed methods of measuring how the brain is using certain neurochemicals, preliminary research suggests that in some ADHD children, the regions involved in controlling attention do not receive normal amounts of certain neurochemicals, while the regions involved in processing sensory information experience an excess of these same chemicals. This observation explains both the ADHD child's difficulties with attentional functioning and his vulnerability to being distracted by seemingly irrelevant sensory information. (Braswell, Bloomquist & Pederson, 1991)

The intelligence of students with ADHD is not affected, and they are capable of abstract thinking. They just can not monitor their behavior and they can not get their school work done. Ben could not do his school work but could give his teachers sophisticated answers to complex questions that required abstract thinking. As his parent, I also found that Ben was capable of understanding adult problems. For example, when I had a problem I could not solve, I could actually go to him for advice. This disorganized youngster was wise beyond his years; he just did not perform well on tasks he was given.

Part of the treatment for persons with neurotransmitter problems is very much like the treatment for diabetes. We give insulin to the diabetic whose pancreas does not produce this essential chemical. We do not expect diabetics to try harder on their own to manage their illness. It is not their fault that they are diabetic; their bodies are not simply lazy or unmotivated. Simply, the diabetic body is incapable of producing insulin on its own. Likewise, some youngsters or adults with ADHD need medical intervention to improve the level of neurotransmitters in their brain. This will allow the students with ADHD to improve their ability to concentrate. The medication for ADHD does not cure the condition, but taking insulin does not cure diabetes, either. The medicine for ADHD and diabetes does allow the person to **manage** a condition for which there is no cure.

Like depression, the actual rate of ADHD in school-aged young people is not known. A conservative figure is five percent, but many researchers feel eight percent is a closer estimate. Until we begin to actively screen for this condition, we will never know.

It is also generally agreed that the condition is more prevalent in boys than in girls. Researchers have generally accepted a ratio of six boys to every one girl, but are now discovering that the ratio for ADHD is more likely three or four boys to every one girl.

WHAT EXPERTS SUGGEST AS EFFECTIVE TREATMENT FOR ADHD

The treatment chosen for any child with ADHD will depend on what characteristics are most prevalent in that child or that which may be most essential to the present or future adjustment of that student. For example, if the child's overactivity presents excessive disturbance to the regular classroom, placement in a smaller, specialized program is an alternative. For the child whose ADHD is less severe, intervention strategies may take the form of additional training for the parents and teachers, or minor alterations to the structure they provide in the home and at school. Effective treatment for ADHD should be a multi-dimensional approach.

Stimulant Medication

"There is overwhelming evidence of the efficacy of stimulant drugs in the treatment of ADHD children" (Barkley, p.95). Although stimulant medication by itself will not take care of all of the problems posed by ADHD and will not cure the condition, it aids school-aged children in their ability to concentrate on academic work. The most common stimulant medications used for ADHD are Ritalin, Dexedrine, and Cylert. Typically, a physician will prescribe the medication to be taken three times a day: early in the morning, before lunch, and mid-afternoon. It takes the medication about 90 minutes to reach optimum efficacy, and it becomes ineffective after four hours. Taking the medication at 7:30 a.m. allows children to be alert for school when it begins at 9:00. Taking it at 11:30 means that after lunch hour, they will again be alert for school when it begins at 1:00. An afternoon dosage will allow children to be alert for any homework they need to complete.

The primary effects of the stimulants (Ritalin, Dexedrine, Cylert) are improved attention span, decreased impulsivity, diminished task-irrelevant activity (especially in structured situations), and generally decreased disruptive behavior in social situations. Secondary effects from these changes appear to be increased compliance to commands and instructions peer acceptance, decreased parent and teacher reprimands, supervision, and punishment; and occasionally, improvement in handwriting. (Russel A. Barkley, pp 95-96)

Some research indicates that 70 percent of children will respond positively to the first medication the physician prescribes. Of the 30 percent who do not respond to the initial drug, two-thirds will respond positively to the second medication tried.

In recent years many doctors have begun to use the antidepressant Wellbutrin for children with ADHD. Wellbutrin is a stimulant medication that is helpful to some persons with depression. This medication has been used successfully by many youngsters with ADHD, and since depression often accompanies learning disabilities, in the years ahead Wellbutrin may prove to be the medication of choice for ADHD.

Doctors find that only a small percentage of children with ADHD are unable to benefit from stimulant medication. Children with high levels of anxiety may be among those youngsters who have adverse reactions to stimulants. In Ben's case, his high level of anxiety may have meant that he would not have responded well to stimulant medicine.

Parent Training in Contingency Management

There are many programs today to help parents become skillful in managing difficult child behavior. Dr. Bradley has developed a program specifically for the parents of children with ADHD. It is based on the work of Forehand and McMahon, but Bradley adds information to help the parent understand the problems posed by ADHD. Bradley's program teaches the parent to use a home token reinforcement system as well as gives instruction on how to deal with behavioral problems occurring in public settings. His program is useful for the parent whose child is between the ages of two and eleven. Of course, the effectiveness of any program is based on the skill, the emotional stability, and the commitment of the parent who uses it. If parents have normal or high intelligence, are blessed with sound health, and are highly determined to help their child, they will be in a good position to do the long, challenging work of teaching their child to control his or her behavior.

Self-Control Training

Children, as well as parents, may benefit from training. Researchers and clinicians have developed a number of approaches, many of which come under the general title of cognitive-behavioral therapy. The underlying principles are to help children recognize a problem, think about it, and come up with a constructive way of dealing with it. Since impulsivity is a primary characteristic of ADHD, children with this condition do not think about what they are going to do before they do it. They certainly do not consider the consequences of their actions. Cognitive-behavioral therapy addresses this issue.

Psychiatrists at the University of Minnesota have developed one of many forms of cognitive-behavioral therapy that may prove to be helpful for children with ADHD. They continuously reinforce the use of a five-step process:

What is taught to students:	**Questions they ask themselves:**
Problem recognition.	*What is the problem?*
Alternative solution thinking - seeing options.	*What is the plan?*
Consequential thinking.	*What will happen?*
Monitoring the effect of the option.	*Is it the best plan?*
Learn to make adjustments.	*How did the plan work?*

Most students think before they act; ADHD youngsters do not. They need formal instruction and continuous practice in this five step problem-solving process developed by Michael Bloomquist Ph.D. and Lauren Braswell Ph.D. These impulsive students need to be taught to stop and think.

1. STOP! WHAT IS THE PROBLEM?

This step requires the child to slow down and recognize the cues which signal the presence of a problem. Children usually need help understanding that cues can come from other people and from their own thoughts, feelings, and bodily sensations.

2. WHAT ARE SOME PLANS?

This step requires the child to generate more than one alternative solution. Children often need help understanding how to brainstorm possible solutions.

3. WHICH IS THE BEST PLAN?

This step requires considering the possible emotional and/or behavioral consequences of each alternative. It is important to help children consider not only the emotional consequences for others, but also how they will feel about themselves if they select a particular alternative.

4. DO THE PLAN.

This step involves acting upon the selected alternative. Sometimes selecting a particular choice requires anticipating or planning around obstacles to successful use of that plan.

5. DID THE PLAN WORK?

This step emphasizes the importance of reviewing the effectiveness of the selected alternative. If the first choice did not work well, then the child selects another choice or follows a back-up plan (Gerald August Ph.D, Deborah Anderson, & Michael Bloomquist Ph.D from the Division of Child & Adolescent Psychiatry, University of Minnesota).

Parent-Adolescent Intervention

In adolescence the ADHD problem not only continues, but there is an emergence of new issues. Developmentally, adolescence is a time when young people learn to become independent of their parent(s). By definition, this means the healthy adolescent will challenge parental authority. When ADHD is added to adolescence, the situation is complex. The approach needed for this age group is different from what was helpful for elementary school children.

The issues of conflict between the ADHD adolescent and parents usually involves "the teenager's acceptance of responsibility (chores, homework, school performance, etc.), disagreements over the teenager's rights and privileges, the social activities in which the teenager may be engaged." (Barkley, p. 97). Dr. Robins has developed a program which focuses on the resolution of conflicts within the families of ADHD teenagers.

Briefly, this approach involves:

1. *training the parents and adolescent in a set of problem-solving steps to be used with each conflict area,*

2. *teaching the parents and adolescent a behavioral style for approaching the use of these steps,*

3. *addressing irrational beliefs that may be held by the parent or adolescent and that may govern their evaluation of and subsequent demands upon each other. (Barkley, p. 97)*

Classroom Management

Not only do the parent and the child need help in learning to cope with ADHD, teachers also need assistance. "Token reinforcement programs, home-based evaluation; reinforcement programs, increased attending by teacher to child compliance, in-class time-out procedures, and behavioral contracts may all be employed in the reduction of ADHD behaviors in the classroom. (Barkley,U. of Massachusett Medical Center)

IS ADHD A HANDICAPPING CONDITION?

Is an attention deficit a handicapping condition? Do children with this disorder qualify for services of some kind?

The Rehabilitation Act of 1973 specifies that a "handicapped individual is any person who: (a) has a physical or mental impairment which substantially limits one or more major life activities; (b) has a record of such an impairment; and (c) is regarded as having such an impairment." (Dr. Phyllis Ann Teeter, 1991)

This definition is so broad that any child with ADHD may or may not be considered handicapped, depending on perspective.

My own perspective is that although some children with ADHD are handicapped, children with a milder condition may not be. However, even mild cases of ADHD left untreated will undoubtedly result in a major lifelong problem for the children and their families; therefore, ADHD is **not** a minor problem. In my own son's case, his "minor" case of ADHD did not allow him to qualify for services. His minor case of ADHD meant he was not defined as handicapped. But his "minor" case substantially contributed to his death. So, although even minor cases of ADHD may not be handicapping, for a small percentage of youngsters, it can be fatal.

Although ADHD is a learning problem, only about 10 percent of children with this condition meet the criteria for learning disabilities. "Parker notes that the 90% who do not qualify are ruled ineligible by the ability/achievement discrepancy that is used by all except four states across the country" (Teeter, 1991, p. 269). Parents of ADHD children want appropriate intervention strategies available for their children. Ch.A.D.D. is a nationwide support group for Children with Attention Deficit Disorder. One of their concerns is that services become available to young people with ADHD. In an age of ever higher federal deficit and greater financial pressures on state, county, and local budgets, many persons who are sympathetic to the suffering of children with ADHD and their families find themselves worried about how additional services can be financed. The children of today may not be able to wait for a balanced budget. They need help now!

LOW-COST, NO-COST PROGRAMS FOR FAMILIES OF ADHD CHILDREN

Those of us most concerned with helping ADHD children may need to look at less ideal, no-cost or low-cost methods of dealing with the large number of children who suffer from this condition. The suggestions I present here are as inexpensive as possible. Some parts are applicable to both ADHD and depression. Since these conditions often go together, a common program will provide the greatest benefit for the greatest number and will eliminate the situation in which the children and his parent are told, "You do not qualify for our program; you do not fit our guidelines." Besides being inexpensive, these suggestions are effective in supporting the children and those who deal with them.

Families of elementary-aged youngsters with ADHD need:

1. *a parent's support group where they can learn the sophisticated behavioral management skills it takes to cope with children with ADHD and where they can obtain the emotional support of others who face the same problem.*

2. *a system of students helping other students that allows them to be useful and reduces their reliance on their parents and teachers to solve problems.*

3. *a social club where any youngster who experiences emotional stress can practice impulse and self-control skills.*

4. *appropriate physical activities.*

5. *continued work on social skills in junior and senior high and beyond.*

Support Group

In a classroom of 30 youngsters, one would expect to find several children with difficulties attending to task and getting their work done. Ch.A.D.D. is a national organization that may be helpful in giving parents guidelines on how to start a local support group. Perhaps your city already has a Ch.A.D.D. Information can be obtained by calling them at (305) 587-3700 in Dallas, Texas or writing them at 1857 N Pine Island Road, #185, Plantation Florida 33322.

If there is no Ch.A.D.D. group in your community, you may want to start one. You could begin by working through the existing parent-teacher organization at your school. They can be helpful in informing parents that you wish to start a group. The teachers, the principal, the school counselor, or the school psychologist may be supportive of your efforts. Once you begin to take some steps in this direction, you may be surprised at how much help you receive. But even if that is not the case, you will know you are doing something to help yourself and your children. This may be the most important source of reinforcement for your efforts.

Once you have joined or founded a local support group, you have the foundation upon which some of the other work can be done. For example, experts recommend parents receive training in contingency management. This skills training can become part of the support group's agenda. It could become an integral part of the meeting, or the group may decide to obtain the training at a separate time. But in either case, the training may be less expensive and perhaps more comfortable in the context of a supportive group. Talking with other parents of ADHD children also gives parents a chance to learn from each other effective ways of utilizing these techniques.

Aside from the skills training, support groups have become extremely popular throughout the country purely for the friendship and uplifting experiences which arise from sharing a common problem. ADHD is a lifelong challenge for families. Parents can easily become discouraged by this problem which never goes away. Many a parent may falsely assume their child's inability to control himself or herself is the child's fault. The support group was put on top of the list of recommendations because it is extremely important to the well-being of the entire family.

Buddy System at School

Since most ADHD youngsters are not going to qualify for the services of a learning disabilities teacher, the question arises: How are these children going to get any individual help? The classroom teacher certainly does not have time to give these children one-to-one assistance throughout the day. ADHD students do need someone to help them stay on course. Who can help? One method is to have other children in the classroom help youngsters with ADHD. This is so important and so valuable to everyone involved that it deserves a thorough discussion. Chapter Five, "Kids Helping Other Kids," describes why this works so well and gives various types of systems. When students are allowed to help each other, the teachers benefit, the parents benefit, the students who do the helping benefit, and the youngster getting the help benefits. All of this is achieved at no cost. If we do not allow students to help each other, we waste our greatest resource.

Special After School Sessions

It is not uncommon for students to belong to Cub Scouts, Boy Scouts, Brownies, and Girl Scouts. Sometimes these club meetings are held in the homes of parents -- sometimes they meet at school. Scout meetings are headed by an adult who teaches youngsters many valuable lessons that will be useful to them throughout life. Would a special club for youngsters with ADHD be that different? The focus of the ADHD club would be to teach the impulse control/self control skills outlined earlier. At the meeting the youngsters could practice the five-steps method described earlier (recognizing problems, listing possible solutions, discussing consequences, using the plan, and evaluating the results.) Like scouts, this club would have projects and recreational activities. The self-control methods would be applied as the ADHD children participate in these activities.

The ADHD club would be smaller in size than a scout troop. It would likely consist of four youngsters. Four is an appropriate number because:

1. *it is two sets of two youngsters -- two groups of athletes for martial arts, racquetball, or other non-team sport.*

2. *four youngsters will fit in most anyone's car (transportation is an important issue).*

3. *four is a large enough number of hyperactive students for any adult to supervise.*

Where are parents going to find someone to head such a group? In the parent support group meeting they will want to brainstorm answers to this question. One of the members of the parent support group may have the time, energy, and skill to head the group. Perhaps a particularly dedicated teacher may take on this commitment. The school system might even budget money for this program. A church leader or adult from a service organization are still other possible resources. Maybe a mental health agency will develop a program. Any of these are viable possibilities, and your support group will likely think of others.

Physical Education

Most students are involved in some kind of sport or physical activity. Team sports are usually frustrating situations for the children with ADHD, and disappointing for their parents. Team sports like baseball can be a disaster for children characterized by inattention, impulsivity, and overactivity. The rules of such games do not require enough physical activity which allows children to be involved on a fairly continuous basis. ADHD children usually benefit most by either individual sports such as swimming, or those that involve interaction with only one other person.

Martial arts training is an excellent choice for these active students. My son joined an inexpensive karate class offered by our local school system. Later he took Aikido at the YMCA. Swimming lessons and opportunities to use the pool are frequently offered both by the public schools and through the YMCA. At the parent support group meeting, parents can discuss which other physical education programs would be available to their children.

The children's ADHD club can incorporate these physical activities into their program. Before going to the gym or the YMCA, the group will use the five-step method to discuss how the children will conduct themselves during the recreational activity (Step 2: What are some plans?), then go ahead and apply the planned solution or solutions to problems during the swimming, martial arts, racquetball, gymnastics, or whatever activity is planned. The adult leader supervises all aspects of the activity, and if problems arise, reinforces the self-control system by praising the children when they use the solutions they planned, or stopping them and repeating the five-step process when problems arise.

Cognitive and Interpersonal Skills Training For Older Students

In my book, The Suicide of My Son, there is a section which outlines cognitive therapy -- a treatment which research has proven to be effective for depression. Cognitive therapy helps older students see the illogical nature of their assumptions, guides them to formulate more logical statements, and helps them apply more reasonable solutions. The cognitive therapy, with its emphasis on homework, could be renamed "Personal Logic" and offered as an academic course in any junior high, senior high, or institution of higher education. Both the 5 percent to 8 percent of older students with ADHD and the 40 percent of older students with mild to severe depression could be served by being allowed to enroll in such a class taught in their school.

ADHD students and depressed students share a common problem with interpersonal skills. Not only has cognitive therapy proven to be effective in the treatment of depression, but interpersonal therapy has also proven to be effective for depressed persons. A class entitled "Interpersonal Skills" would be of help to depressed students and the ADHD population. My preference would be to join the two classes into one; perhaps calling it "Personal Logic and Interpersonal Skills."

What about the cost? Perhaps the school board may want to look carefully at the courses they now offer and ask themselves if this class is not a higher priority than some of their current class offerings. Since nearly 40 percent of the older students may be experiencing some form of depression, and since depression causes a general reduction in the ability to concentrate, a class offering some hope in lifting depression could be of enormous benefit to the students' general performance. Classes would be offered as an elective to older students. It could be open to any student who wishes to take it. Not only would a depressed student or a student with ADHD benefit from the class, but so would anyone interested in personal growth. Research indicates that anyone could benefit from programs which teach more rational thinking and improved interpersonal behaviors. Furthermore, taking the class more than once in their academic careers is not unreasonable for persons with ADHD. Don't we all take classes over and over again on a more advanced level? How many years did you take a class designed to develop skills in reading and writing?

Medication and Private Therapy

My last suggestion does cost some money, although insurance may help to cover the costs. Parents need not be afraid to allow their children to take medications for their condition. The more we learn about the physical nature of the brain, the more we will see the logic behind their use. Choose a doctor you can talk to, and someone you respect.

Some people do not wish to join a group but are willing to seek private therapy. The key to choosing a good therapist is the same as for finding a good doctor. Perhaps Ch.A.D.D., a friend or a physician can recommend someone. Choose a therapist you are comfortable with and someone you respect.

Chapter 5

Portrait of an ADHD Child

Do your children have an attention deficit disorder or are they just normally active youngsters? Is the disappointing performance in school their fault for not trying hard enough, or is there actually something medically wrong? Are the problems they have getting along with siblings and playmates your fault as a parent? What does attention deficit disorder actually look like in the everyday life of youngsters? Parents may not always ask these questions out loud. They might just see their children having problems and wonder why they behave the way they do.

Hyperactivity has been the part of ADHD which typically causes the most disruption at home and in school. ADHD children who are not particularly hyperactive often go undiagnosed. The concentration problem is troublesome to them and to their conscientious parents, but since they do not cause classroom disturbance, they usually do not get the attention from the school they need. Parents who want to know if their children have this very common problem, and teachers who are searching to find the reason some of their students do not do well deserve some answers.

SIX BASIC RESEARCH FINDINGS

Much has been written in recent years by scientists about ADHD. The common ground all researchers and physicians have in describing children with ADHD consists of the following six generalizations:

(1) The inattention, impulsivity and overactivity of these children is not what parents and teachers would expect to find for children of this age.

We expect toddlers to have short attention spans. We do not expect three and four year olds to think before they act or to have a good understanding of the consequences of their behavior. We know very young children have difficulty sitting still for periods of time. But as children enter school, the ability to pay attention, control their impulses, and sit quietly has developed to some extent. Children with ADHD do not have the ability to do what we expect of children that age.

(2) Children with ADHD do not have the ability to regulate their behavior to fit the situation.

When children are on the playground or in the gymnasium, they probably are running around and making lots of noise. But when recess is over or the gym teacher blows the whistle to stop, most children can calm down. ADHD children have difficulty stopping. It is not because they are bad or are deliberately flaunting the rules; it is simply that they do not have the ability to regulate their behavior.

(3) ADHD children have had problems with inattention, impulsivity, and overactivity ever since they were born.

Some parents of ADHD children describe them as being especially active as infants. Other parents do not recall any particular difficulties until they are 3 or 4 years old. Still other parents may not discover any difficulty until they enter school. If these children are particularly bright, and the attention deficit is not severe, they may not experience problems with school until the work requires enormous concentration. Highly intelligent youngsters with a mild case of ADHD may not have difficulty meeting the demands of school until sometime in junior high, high school, or even in college. Although the problem may only concern students at some later point, they actually had the condition since birth.

(4) Pervasiveness of problems between settings and caregivers (e.g. children usually have problems getting their assignments done no matter what class it is or who the teacher is.)

Getting school assignments completed and handed in on time is one of the salient characteristics of students with ADHD. These children will likely have this problem not just in first or second grade, but in all their school years, regardless of the teacher. Some teachers provide a structure that helps disorganized students stay as organized as they can. Consequently, there will be some variations on the extent their problem manifests itself from teacher to teacher, as illustrated by Ben's story. But in general, ADHD children have difficulty concentrating on work at school, and they also struggle to complete it at home.

(5) ADHD is a chronic problem.

Children may be able to learn coping strategies that help them manage their difficulties, but the problem never goes away. Like children with diabetes, children with ADHD may take medication which helps their body function more effectively. And, like children with diabetes, both they and their parents need to learn to manage the medical condition. The parents of diabetic children learn about proper diet and the youngster develops routine eating habits. The parents of ADHD children learn behavioral management skills, and the youngster develops a routine of following a behavioral program. At this writing there is no cure for ADHD. There is only the beginning of understanding it, some methods of coping with it, and the enormous need to be supportive to the child who has this condition.

(6) The symptoms of ADHD are not the result of other medical conditions.

When my son was diagnosed as ADHD, he went through a series of other medical tests. He had an EEG to rule out epilepsy or other neurological conditions. The results were negative. He was given an intelligence test to rule out whether or not his difficulties with school were due to low intelligence. He had normal intelligence. He was seen by a psychologist and a psychiatrist to rule out certain types of psychopathology such as autism or schizophrenia. His inattention, impulsivity, and over-activity were not caused by those medical conditions. There is one medical condition, however, that is sometimes associated with ADHD -- problems with neurotransmitters. Ben did have a complex depressive condition. Not all persons with depression have ADHD, but since both ADHD and depression are most likely to be caused by problems with neurotransmitters, it is not surprising that some students with ADHD also have depression. Research indicates that perhaps the majority of students with learning problems also have depression. Whether the depression causes the attention deficit, or the attention deficit and subsequent continuous failures in other aspects of life cause the depression, no one can say. This continues to be a question asked by researchers and may be answered in the years ahead. But, for whatever reason, we see depression and ADHD together. It is not surprising that depression -- the common cold of mental difficulties and the number one public health problem in the world -- may occur simultaneously with ADHD. (Russel A. Barkley, University of Massachusetts Medical Center)

INCONSISTENCIES IN BEHAVIOR OF YOUNG PEOPLE WITH ADHD

Different Behaviors in Different Settings

ADHD can be a baffling condition. The children with ADHD will not show the symptoms of inattention (inability to concentrate initially or to sustain concentration), impulsivity (lack of ability to monitor their behaviors), and heightened activity to the same extent in all situations or environments. For example, many ADHD youngsters can perform fairly well on standardized achievement tests when done in a one-to-one setting, but the same child's performance will be dramatically different on a similar standardized achievement test if it is given in a group setting such as in a regular classroom.

Expect inconsistencies from ADHD students, and refrain from making assumptions of how they "should" be able to function in the classroom based on observations or tests conducted outside of their normal environment. Any test or observation done in an atypical environment is ecologically invalid. They tell us nothing about what these children are actually able to do in their everyday lives.

The importance of refraining from using tests conducted in unusual environments is so great that it is worth taking a close look at what was done in Ben's case. As described earlier, I thought Ben had a learning disability, and I wanted him to get services in the school from a learning disabilities teacher so that he could improve. I requested an evaluation by the Learning Disabilities (LD) teacher.

Ben's evaluation was done in October of 1984, early in fourth grade. He was given the Woodcock-Johnson Psycho-educational Battery, a test made up of many subtests measuring both aptitude (ability) and achievement. The aptitude scores reflected what Ben was capable of doing. Ben's aptitude in reading was 5th grade 8th month, and in math was 4th grade 6th month. The achievement score, on the other hand, told what Ben's actual performance was in these subjects. His actual achievement in reading was 5th grade 0 month, and math was 3rd grade 7th month.

When Ben's aptitude (what he was capable of doing), was compared to his achievement (what his actual performance was in those subjects) his aptitude was approximately one year higher than his achievement in both reading and math.

The Woodcock-Johnson Battery is an individually administered test. The LD guidelines in our state do not include any comparison of this individually administered test with a classroom administered achievement test. This is unfortunate because we could learn a great deal from such a comparison. The California Achievement Test, a group test, was also given that year to all the fourth graders. It happened to be given at approximately the same time Ben took his individual test. Ben's scores on that classroom administered test were: Reading 3rd grade 2nd month, Math 1st grade 9th month, Language Expression 1st grade 7th month.

Thus, in October of fourth grade (4th grade 2nd month) when Ben was given the group standardized achievement test in the classroom setting, he received an average score of 2nd grade 1st month -- well below average. Whereas, when given individual attention during testing, Ben showed an aptitude that was much higher and much more typical for his grade level. This tells a lot about how children with attention deficit disorder function in the classroom versus how they function in small, less distracted environments with the benefit of individual attention.

The state-mandated guidelines in Minnesota for children's entrance into a learning disabilities program requires a wide difference between the scores children receive on an aptitude or intelligence test and the scores they receive on an achievement test. The intelligence test must show a much higher score than what the achievement test shows they have actually learned. Individual testing results are always used.

But is not the group-administered test done in the classroom setting more indicative of what children typically do in the classroom? Should not those test scores be taken into consideration when looking at the difference between children's aptitude and classroom performance? What better way of seeing the difference between what children are capable of doing and what they actually can do in the classroom than by comparing an aptitude test with an achievement test given in the classroom by the teacher? Wouldn't this be especially important for children who have a problem with concentration, which is an attention deficit?

On Ben's evaluation form, the following was added:

> When Ben's cognitive scores in reading and math were compared with the achievement scores in reading and math, he received a score indicating below average functioning. This means the deficit is not sufficient to qualify him for learning disabilities help. The finding of this evaluation is that he does not meet the eligibility requirement for services as learning disabled.

Already typed on the form at the time of the parent/teacher conference was the statement, "Based on the above information, as a Child Study Team member, I conclude that this student does not have a Specific Learning Disability." Following this statement, there was a place for each of us to sign.

During the conference, I never felt my opinion was sought. I was not listened to, but talked at. The conference only served to weaken my confidence in my own common sense. I left the meeting thinking I was wrong about my own observation and foolish in thinking that Ben had a learning problem. I found the experience humiliating and confusing.

In the spring of Ben's fifth grade year when he was crying and expressing disappointment with his school performance, I became committed to more evaluation of his learning problems. I requested he again be evaluated for learning disability services from the school system. Ben was re-evaluated by the LD teacher in May of 1986. At the end of the month we met with her, the school psychologist, one of his fifth-grade teachers, a sixth grade teacher he would have the following September, and the principal. Her findings from individualized testing were: Reading 8th grade 8th month, Math 6th grade 3rd month, and Written Language 6th grade 6th month. These scores were again much higher than he would receive on a California Achievement Test given in the classroom.

I had the same feeling from this meeting as I had from the one a year and a half earlier. Information was presented, but there was little encouragement for us to speak. I got the impression our second request for an evaluation was a nuisance to them. We were again expected to go along with the consensus that Ben did not have a specific learning disability. There would again be no help for Ben through the schools. Learning disabilities programs, as they are currently set up in many school systems, require the students to "qualify for services." They may be designed more for students with problems like dyslexia than youngsters with ADHD.

Ben's experience with the learning disabilities program at school underscores two important points.

1. *ADHD youngsters are inconsistent in their performance. To expect them to be consistent is to misunderstand their condition.*

2. *ADHD youngsters generally will not qualify for services of a special teacher. Parents and regular classroom teachers must rely on their own skills and the help of peers as a buddy/tutor to give them the support they need to function in the classroom.*

Situational Variation

ADHD children can be baffling, not only because they are inconsistent in different settings, but also because they can be inconsistent in similar settings. Evidence in the literature supports this. For example, two classrooms with 30 students are similar settings, but the ADHD child may act very differently in one class depending on how the teacher has structured the environment. ADHD students need structure but not rigidity. The teacher who provides comfortable but substantial structure goes a long way in helping ADHD students.

When I think of this, I remember Ben's seventh grade math teacher. The first day of school, Ben came home almost panic stricken because this teacher made it clear that the students in the class **were** going to be organized and **were** going to follow the rules. My son knew his general inability to be organized, and following rigid rules made these demands seem overwhelming. But this gifted teacher also provided the **means**, the structure, by which even my son could comply. This teacher expected his students to control themselves, but he also treated them as responsible ladies and gentlemen. The combination of structure and respect allowed my son to function better in this classroom than he would have done in classrooms run by teachers with too loose or too rigid a structure. Ben's seventh grade math teacher provided exactly what ADHD students need.

Another important variable for ADHD youngsters is the individual who is asking them to perform a task. Some research indicates ADHD students often respond with more attention and control to their fathers than to their mothers. Parents of these students can fall into a trap of blaming each other for their inability to handle them, but it is not clear exactly what factor may be operating here. It could be that these children perceive their mother as less likely to enforce the natural consequences of their behavior. Without experiencing these consequences, they are less likely to comply or learn how to function with her. Another possibility may be that mothers are more likely to rely on the use of verbal rules. In the next section, an explanation is given for why ADHD students are not rule-governed. This difference in the child's behavior towards the mother or the father may relate to a general inability to function under verbal reprimands.

It is my hypothesis that parents, male or female, who come to recognize the need to assist the youngsters in problem solving and who use contingency-based strategies to provide natural consequences for inappropriate behavior will go a long way in helping their ADHD children.

Youngsters with ADHD will also function differently in similar settings when the type of activity they are asked to perform is different. Asking them to read a chapter in social studies and answer the questions at the end is a very different task from asking them to play a social studies game with a buddy or on a computer. Similarly, standing out in left field waiting for a fly ball is a very different task than practicing karate or playing racquetball with a partner. ADHD students need fairly continuous stimulation in order to maintain their attention. Activities that demand concentration through long periods of time are more than they can handle. Again, some flexibility is required on the part of parents and teachers to give them tasks they can handle. This may take the form of giving them an alternative assignment in the classroom and avoiding some team sports such as baseball or any sport in which they must wait their turn or be inactive for periods of time. Individual sports like swimming, track, or martial arts should be emphasized.

RULE GOVERNING BEHAVIOR

In this portrait of what an ADHD child is like, it is important to include a characteristic which may summarize another overriding problem. Dr. Russell A. Barkley has hypothesized that besides their problems with inattention, impulsivity, and over activity, ADHD students may have an additional deficit in rule-governing behavior. He writes, "*rule-governing* behavior refers to the ability of language (commands, directions, instructions, descriptions, etc.) or other symbol systems to serve as discriminative stimuli for behavior." In his many years of experience with these youngsters, Dr. Barkley finds that ADHD students have great difficulty complying with rules given to them by their parents and teachers. This inability to comply with what is asked of them may take one or several forms. The youngster may not follow the rules or obey the command when they are first given. Or they may begin by following the rules, but after hours, days, or weeks, are not able to continue. Or they may comply with the rules in a way that is unacceptable.

Dr. Barkley states that much of the research done with children with ADHD which attempts to test attention and impulsivity actually involves "rule-governing behavior" in that the child is asked to do a task by the tester. Their research has always found that ADHD youngsters have "difficulties in sustaining compliance to task instructions, especially when the task is boring and there are few or no consequences for doing so."

Dr. Barkley has also found that ADHD students have poor problem-solving abilities both in school settings and in social situations. He points out that problem solving is a type of rule-governing behavior. When a child problem-solves, he thinks of several questions, rules or possibilities which, if followed, lead to a solution. ADHD students have difficulty either in clearly seeing the problems which confront them, or in seeing the options they would have, or in carrying through with the solutions that are possible. Whatever the cause (and they may have difficulty with all three), ADHD students need assistance in problem solving in every situation in life.

Dr. Barkley hypothesizes that ADHD students are "contingency-shaped" rather than "rule-governed." By this he means their behavior is dependent more on the consequences their behavior has. Their behavior is strongly affected by the rewards it produces or its positive natural consequences. For example, if lying about something means they get out of doing something they do not want to do, then it is a rewarding behavior. The rule against lying means very little to the ADHD child, not because they are deliberately defiant, but because they are not rule-governed. Shaming an ADHD child for his lack of rule-governed orientation is like shaming a blond or red-haired child because they do not have brown hair. Instead, children with ADHD may be helped by frequent praise or token reinforcements for behavior that does comply with requests, and by providing natural consequences (having the consequences really fit the transgression).

Ben's toilet training is an example of the lack of "rule-governing" and the use of contingency-based training. My daughter, Caroline, was able to learn the rule: use the toilet, keep your clothing dry. After a few days of training with the use of praise and edible reinforcement, she understood the rule and could follow it. Ben, on the other hand, understood what a toilet was for and wanted to use it, but failed even though we were trying to teach him the rule and were providing praise and edible reinforcement when he succeeded. It was only when there were negative consequences that he learned to refrain from wetting himself. When our teaching was contingency based, he learned quickly.

MEDICAL CRITERIA FOR ADHD

ADHD is diagnosed by a physician rather than by school personnel. The Diagnostic Symptoms Manual (DSM IV) gives fourteen possible symptoms associated with the condition. Although their list of symptoms is not perfect, and there are many criticisms of the scientific basis of the items on the list, they do add to our portrait of a typical youngster with ADHD. Here are the guidelines used by physicians:

Diagnostic criteria for Attention Deficit / Hyperactivity Disorder

A. Either (1) or (2):

(1) six (or more) of the following symptoms of inattention have persisted for at least 6 months to a degree that is maladaptive and inconsistent with developmental level:

Inattention

(a) often fails to give close attention to details or makes careless mistakes in schoolwork, work, or other activities

(b) often has difficulty sustaining attention in tasks or play activities

(c) often does not seem to listen when spoken to directly

(d) often does not follow through on instructions and fails to finish schoolwork, chores, or duties in the workplace (not due to oppositional behavior or failure to understand instructions)

(e) often has difficulty organizing tasks and activities

(f) often avoids, dislikes, or is reluctant to engage in tasks that require sustained mental effort (such as schoolwork or homework)

(g) often loses things necessary for tasks or activities (e.g., toys, school assignments, pencils, books, or tools)

(h) is often easily distracted by extraneous stimuli

(i) is often forgetful in daily activities

(2) six (or more) of the following symptoms of hyperactivity-impulsivity have persisted for at least 6 months to a degree that is maladaptive and inconsistent with developmental level:

Hyperactivity

(a) often fidgets with hands or feet or squirms in seat

(b) often leaves seat in classroom or in other situations in which remaining seated is expected

(c) often runs about or climbs excessively in situations in which it is inappropriate (in adolescents or adults, may be limited to subjective feelings of restlessness)

(d) often has difficulty playing or engaging in leisure activities quietly

(e) is often "on the go" or often acts as if "driven by a motor"

(f) often talks excessively

Impulsivity

(g) often blurts out answers before questions have been completed

(h) often has difficulty awaiting turn

(i) often interrupts or intrudes on others (e.g., butts into conversations or games)

B. Some hyperactive-impulsive or inattentive symptoms that caused impairment were present before age 7 years.

C. Some impairment from the symptoms is present in two or more settings (e.g., at school [or work] and at home).

D. There must be clear evidence of clinically significant impairment in social, academic, or occupational functioning.

E. The symptoms do not occur exclusively during the course of a Pervasive Developmental Disorder, Schizophrenia, or other Psychotic Disorder and are not better accounted for by another mental disorder (e.g., Mood Disorder, Anxiety)

Ben, as an example

Did Ben's classroom behavior fit that description? The learning disabilities teacher was required to do a classroom observation of Ben as part of her evaluation. In the report she did early in his fourth grade year she wrote,

> Ben was observed during an independent work time. During his independent work time, Ben was to work on spelling and then math.... About one-third of the time he was observed, he was off task doing such things as taking a pencil apart and fixing it, playing with a wad of paper, making faces at another boy, pushing his cheeks or turning around and talking. Teacher reminded him to get his pencil put away and get to work. During the 10 minutes he spent doing math, he got 8 examples finished. When on task, he worked very slowly. He knew how to do his math but could not seem to get going. At times, his writing forms were not accurate.
>
> He has the ability to do average to above-average work but is off task too much of the time to complete his assigned papers. He knows what to do, but can't keep at it.

When she evaluated Ben in the spring of fifth grade, she again observed his performance in the classroom. Her report stated:

> Ben was to work on individual assignments that were late and not in. He had lots of work (15 out) but about half the time he was off task -- playing with a mechanical toy, a rubber band, walking about room, talking to those around him: he'd get a booklet to use but almost immediately it was returned unused. He never asked for help from his regular teacher or the student teacher -- many did. He was on task less than 50% of time.

She did a second observation two days later and wrote,

> He was doing math from text book -- did finish it -- worked mixed with talking, walking around, rocking desk, etc. Put math away. Took four minutes to get to spelling. Remained on task. He was not disruptive at any time; did not ask for help for his assignment; was easily distracted. In oral reading there were very few errors.

Does Ben's classroom behavior fit what one would expect to find from a child with an attention deficit disorder -- inattention, impulsive, hyperactive? Clearly it does. But in fairness to the LD teacher, it is not her job to make a medical diagnosis. The prevailing system at the time Ben was in school handled learning problems caused by anatomy (dyslexia), but did not handle learning problems caused by brain chemistry (ADHD).

Was Ben's behavior outside the classroom what you would expect from a child with ADHD? Youngsters with this disorder engage in dangerous behaviors that can cause harm to themselves or others. Ben had a broken collar bone, a concussion and a broken arm -- all within approximately 18 months between the ages of four and a half and six.

When Dr. Gerald T. August mentioned in one of his lectures that the child you read about who suffers a serious injury or who drowns is sometimes an ADHD child, his remark reminded me of the time Ben almost drowned. It was Christmas time and he was in third grade. The teachers in our school district went on strike that year, but since we had plans to go to Florida we used it as an opportunity to have an especially long vacation in the sun. We spent lots of time on the beach. Ben loved to jump into the waves, while I sat on shore with a book, looking up from time to time to see where he was.

Suddenly, something told me Ben had been swept into the ocean. I stood up and could not see him anywhere. My husband had just gotten back from a walk and was as concerned as I was. We felt helpless and panicked. Much to our relief, a young boy had pulled Ben from the waves.

There were many other incidents in which Ben did or could have gotten hurt. One winter night before Ben's fourteenth birthday, we heard tramping on our roof. My husband and I were in our bedroom, lazily watching the 6 o'clock news, when we heard the noise of footsteps overhead. It was Ben jumping off the roof into a snow bank. That kind of behavior may not be typical of most students, but it is the kind of thing a young person with ADHD might do. Ben's dangerous behaviors fortunately never hurt anyone else, but it was always a real possibility, especially as he got older.

DEVELOPMENTAL COURSE AND PREDICTORS OF OUTCOME

In any portrait of typical youngsters with ADHD, these questions arise: What does the condition look like in different age groups? Are there signs of this condition well before the child enters school? Although every child is different and no single description will be universally valid, there are some general observations which help to show the course this condition can take.

Infancy

The characteristics of infants who later are recognized as having ADHD are similar to many of the characteristics of youngsters who later are diagnosed as having either bipolar depression or one of the other conditions caused by problems with neurotransmitters. Many ADHD infants have problems eating and difficulty sleeping. Excessive activity, difficult temperament, and negative mood have all been observed in infants who later develop ADHD. When a child has both depression and ADHD, it is difficult to say which of these symptoms are caused by one condition and which symptoms are caused by the other. What can be said is that both of these conditions share a common factor: improper functioning of neurotransmitters of the brain. Perhaps it is not surprising that infants with either or both conditions would have similar symptoms.

Preschool

By the time the child reaches the age of three, the characteristics of inattention, impulsivity, and over-activity are seen in half of the children who later are diagnosed as having ADHD. Many parents find themselves child-proofing the home rather than continually saying "No" or "Stop that" to the child. Child-proofing is also a safety issue, since youngsters who have dangerous behavior can cause injury to themselves.

Some parents report that the preschool years are an especially trying time. If their children's behavior is particularly disruptive to others, the parents may be asked to remove them from the day care or nursery school setting. Because my own child received day care from a tolerant and loving older couple, preschool was not as difficult for us as it is for many others. For the parent who stays at home to raise their children, the preschool years can be an especially demanding and difficult time.

School Age

By age six, 90 percent of ADHD students are recognized as problematic by their parents or teacher, although unfortunately they may not be properly diagnosed. In the classroom, they will have difficulty staying on task, following classroom rules, or handing in assignments on time. Sitting still and paying attention to the teacher's direction is a challenge for the ADHD youngster. They will also have problems getting along with peers. Their emotional makeup and lack of positive social skills may cause other children to avoid them. It is not uncommon for ADHD children to have few friends or to have friends who are also having problems. Stealing and property destruction are not uncommon for children with ADHD. Most ADHD children have low self-esteem.

Dr. Barkley points out other challenges parents of ADHD children encounter:

> With exposure to broader social situations (school, community, public places), ADHD children pose even greater management difficulties for their parents, particularly in unsupervised situations. At an age when children can often be trusted to follow appropriate social rules when outside of parental supervision, ADHD children are often described by their parents as being

incapable of being trusted when alone. Parents may now have difficulty getting baby-sitters to sit with these children because of the history of chronic behavioral problems under such conditions. Parents often find themselves spending most of the children's waking day supervising their activities. They may even come to spend less time with the children in recreational pursuits because of frequent management problems posed under such conditions.

Classroom behavior problems may take the form of being disruptive and having little self control in situations where the teacher is not directly supervising, such as the hallways, playgrounds, and school buses. Due to their inability to pay attention while the teacher is instructing or in completing the work which would help them learn, ADHD children may not learn fundamental skills. If they are exceptionally bright, they may learn as much as their peers, although perhaps not as much as they could with their potential. For children of average intelligence with ADHD, or youngsters with a severe case of ADHD, academic skills will not be adequate for their grade. Furthermore, the difference between what they can do and what their peers can do will widen with each passing year. Lastly, as they progress through the grades, the type of work that is required demands higher and higher levels of sustained concentration. The need for intervention in the academic area for these students is abundantly clear.

This portrait of ADHD children makes it clear that the condition is difficult, baffling, and frustrating for everyone concerned. The children, the parents, the classroom teacher all deserve more help, less stress, and tasks that are manageable. The chapters which follow will continue to focus on what can be done in our era of fiscal budget restraints to cope with this extremely common condition.

Chapter 6

Kids Helping Other Kids

The greatest problem facing most parents and teachers is finding the emotional resource and the time to work with children who have difficulty with school. Parents are tired at the end of the day. Ben used to look at me and remark, "You work so hard during the day, and then you come home and have problems with your kids." He realized that it was difficult for parents to deal with a disorganized child who did not have his school work done. Teachers, too, have many demands on their time. Can we expect them to develop an individual learning program to meet each single child's needs? Probably not. But the individual problems of the child still need to be addressed.

I have written that the essence of work on self-esteem with young people is to allow them to see themselves as an asset rather than a liability. Instead of seeing the things they do as meaningless or worthless, but as helpful and valuable to others, there is some chance of them having a reason to feel good about themselves. Rather than giving a list of what teachers can do to help students with problems, and a list of what parents can do to help their child, I'd like to focus on what students can do to help each other.

My enthusiasm for this comes once again from my life experience. In the schoolhouse of my childhood, students helped each other in three separate ways. First, each day a number of eighth graders came to listen to the first and second graders read. This was a very simple program of older student tutors helping all the younger students, giving them added opportunities for supervised reading. Second, in the middle and upper grades, teachers made use of peer tutoring. Small groups of students read to each other. Lastly, there was specialized help for individual students. For example, when I was in seventh grade, my teacher teamed me up with a sixth grader who was having reading problems. Since I had reading problems myself, this was especially important for me.

The benefits of peer tutoring are numerous and well documented by research. The data clearly shows the double benefits of tutoring. Both the students being tutored and the students doing the tutoring demonstrate improvement. These improvements shown are in both the quantity and the accuracy of their work. Furthermore, students improve both academically and socially. Here are just some of the many benefits of this low cost or no cost system.

WHY THIS IS AN IMPORTANT SOURCE OF HELP

1. All students can get help.

The current program of special help for some students is controversial. The present system of testing students to determine if they qualify for help is expensive and necessarily excludes many students. The parents of youngsters who need help but do not qualify are frustrated, and may feel discriminated against. Even those parents whose children do get help still get frustrated with the system. One mother described this experience. Her child had problems reading, and would actually qualify for help when she was failing a class. When the child got help, she could get an A or a B in the course, but when the grades improved, the child would become disqualified from receiving continuing help. Without help, the child would again begin to fail and would again qualify for help. This mother was rightfully cynical of a program that does not respond to the continuing needs of the student.

Special help usually focuses only on academic problems. Most students with mild or moderate emotional problems do not qualify for special services. With peer teaching no one needs to be excluded. Teachers can choose to have all children involved in some aspects of peer tutoring, and can emphasize this system for particular students who especially benefit from it. Discrimination is eliminated.

2. *The tutor benefits from tutoring.*

The tutor is helped in at least two separate ways. He comes to understand the daily lessons more thoroughly when he has to explain it to someone else, and his self-esteem is enhanced from doing the really important work of helping fellow students. In some classrooms, all students are given the opportunity to be the tutor. The class can be divided into small groups, and the role of tutor is rotated among the students.

It is important to remember that not only the especially capable students can act as tutors, but students who have received specialized help themselves would be good candidates. For example, a dyslexic fourth grade child could help a second grader who also has reading blindness. The older child's own experience naturally gives him insight into the younger child's difficulty. It can make him an excellent and sensitive tutor. The younger child, in turn, looks up to the older child who has the problem but is working to deal with it. Experts on ADHD also recommend allowing the child with ADHD to teach what he has recently learned to a peer or to a younger student in another class.

3. The children receiving the tutoring are helped.

The children getting the help benefit in a number of ways. Hearing an explanation for a second time or in a slightly different way is helpful. But peer tutors can help each other not only by teaching, but by checking each other's assignments for accuracy and by reviewing material for mastery. Students who otherwise would not have succeeded can now do so. Students helped by peers sometimes take the lessons more to heart than when they are given them by an adult. Some students relate to each other better than to an adult. Any youngster who mistrusts adults may be more open to listening to a fellow student or a tutor a few years older than he.

4. Children do not need to wait for help.

When students are helping each other there are a number of teachers in the room, not just one. Children with questions do not need to waste time standing in line or stopping their work until the teacher can get to them. They do not have to feel discouraged about the long drawn-out process which keeps some children from asking for help, especially students who need help frequently. Children begin to see each other as resources.

5. Teaching can be fun for students.

Teaching can be just plain fun. Many of us liked to play school when we were young, just as much as we liked to play house. For any student whose previous experience with school has not been fun, interacting in a peer learning situation can make a big difference to change his attitude. When peer teaching is used, the student can not only do his regular school work, but can play one of the many reading games after a work session is over. Since students get more work done, and get it done more accurately when they help each other, there is more time to do things like playing games that enhance skills. For some students, peer teaching can go a long way in changing their whole attitude towards the learning process.

6. Parents deserve a break.

Parents deserve some assistance with the task of helping their children. I helped my child with homework several hours each night; a lot to expect of any parent. When the child has a problem with school, it automatically means that the parent also has a problem with school. I am not saying that peer teaching always works perfectly. Nothing worked perfectly for Ben. But, it is a system that would allow more students to get some help, and it is a method that takes an unnecessary burden off busy parents.

Increasingly, I see parents doing what I did: working all day at a job, trying to keep the house in order, and spending hours helping their child with homework. Students helping other students would give everyone, including overworked but sympathetic adults, a much needed and deserved break. It would also give the tutoring student a sense of purpose and accomplishment, which many students lack.

7. *Cooperation reduces losers.*

Classrooms that produce competition among students can be exciting and enjoyable for capable students who view themselves as winners. Competition is disheartening for less capable students who begin to view themselves as losers. It creates an atmosphere of vying for a goal that only a few can achieve. Cooperation creates an atmosphere of friends working together for mutual benefit. What kind of environment do we want our children to have? In which kind of environment would we rather work?

Cooperation is the way any successful business functions. Sound businesses need to be efficient. Cooperation produces efficiency. There can be some friendly rivalry between teams, but there has to be cooperation within the team. Classrooms do not have to eliminate all forms of competition, but if they limit the use of competition to situations that are both fair and fun, there can be balance between cooperation and competition that will prevent demoralization of the youngsters who constantly have difficulty.

8. Cooperation meets the needs of today.

Another benefit for student cooperation is that it is perhaps the most realistic way of thinking about the problems currently facing our world. We are becoming aware that to preserve our global environment while sustaining our economy we must have the cooperation of all the nations of the world. Cooperation among nations is essential on all levels. Gone are the days when competition by itself benefits anyone. An atmosphere of mutual cooperation for the benefit of all, while retaining competition when appropriate, is the way the world works. It can also be the way our classrooms work.

Competition in the classroom does not meet the emotional needs of our young people. Today's students are living in a world of ever-increasing change and stress. Few children are blessed with high intelligence and the total absence of problems. Few young people have the same family home throughout childhood, have all the emotional support they need, or have economic security. Many students have health problems. Today's children need all the emotional support and help they can get. In practical terms, this translates into peer support -- cooperation rather than competition.

With all the benefits to students, teachers, and parents that peer tutoring has, there is no reason to not use it. It is a no cost system. The students produce more and better work in an atmosphere that provides emotional support. In addition, the use of peer tutoring does a better job of preparing our students for responsible adult living than does an atmosphere exclusive of competition. The only question is how do we effectively train children to be good peer tutors?

TEACHING YOUNGSTERS TO BE PEER TUTORS

If we recognize the value of using peer tutoring for all children and especially for children with difficulty, we may want to implement these programs into the academic lives of youngsters as soon as possible. There was an interesting study that showed how first graders were taught tutoring skills. What is most interesting about this research is that the teacher did not train those first graders; older students taught the first graders how to teach each other. A summary of the program says:

> In an innovative study, Jason, Frasure and Ferone (1981) used a classroom of eighth graders to train, systematically, a class of first graders in effective peer tutoring behaviors (presenting questions, corrective feedback, and contingent social reinforcement). Evaluations indicated that the eighth graders successfully taught these teaching skills to first graders and that peer tutoring resulted in significant academic and behavioral gains for the first graders.

From this we can conclude that the most efficient way to train lots of students to become tutors is to begin by training the oldest and the brightest students in the proper peer tutoring behavior, and then have them in turn teach the younger students and students who have problems learning. By being efficient, the program could cost little or no money and would mean that only one teacher would have to be involved in the initial training of the older students.

If teachers at different grade levels are interested in using peer tutoring, the school can take advantage of the efficiency of scale that having older students do the training can offer. But even when there are no older students to do the training, any classroom teacher can be efficient in training peer tutors. Training a small group of most capable students and then relying on them to train the other students has the same effect.

SPECIAL CONSIDERATIONS FOR ADHD

Peer tutoring helps all children. The child with an attention deficit disorder is especially in need of help; so is the child who may be particularly difficult for peers to work with. These children lack social skills as well as concentration, so they may not be the most popular children in the room. Not only do adults find the ADHD youngster a challenge to teach, but peers may also.

The teacher might want to choose a tutor who is highly efficient at getting his own work done and has lots of time to help the ADHD youngster. Another possibility is to have a number of children as tutors. One plan would be to have one child tutor the ADHD child on Monday, another child be the helper on Tuesday, and so forth throughout the week. An alternative is to have different tutors for different subjects. For example, Mary is the math tutor, John is the reading tutor, Bill is the spelling tutor, etc. In some classrooms, teachers may prefer to have a child from a higher grade come in at various times to help children in a lower grade. Individual teachers will want to experiment with these plans, or come up with plans of their own to create something that feels comfortable for everyone.

Chapter 7

Reducing Stress For Teachers As Well As Students

Every time I pick up an article or book dealing with problems affecting children, there is always the list of all the things teachers and parents can do to help. I ask, "Where is the list of things we can **stop** doing?" In my years as a teacher, it seemed as if every time there was a problem with a youngster it automatically became the role of the school to fix it. It was as if some "pie-in-the-sky" intellectual came up with a theory and it was up to the already overworked classroom teacher to actually do the work. I wondered who was ever going to open the door to making teaching less complex and stressful? Can't we design things to be less complicated rather than more?

TEACHERS DESERVE A BREAK

When we ask teachers to work with ADHD students -- children whose problems concentrating and getting their work done is difficult to manage -- it is essential that teachers spend enough time with the child in order that they:

1. *have a chance to understand the problem,*

2. *can discover a method that works, is manageable and comfortable for both the teacher and the children,*

3. *can bond emotionally with the child, allowing both the teacher and the student to develop a commitment to the success of their efforts, and*

4. *can reap the benefits of a successful program and thus experience a sense of accomplishment when completion of school work is less of a hassle for their students.*

What I am proposing is a step in reducing stress for both teachers and their students while allowing them to keep their pupils for a slightly longer period over time. We can reduce stress when everyone is not being continually asked to change. It is the pace of continuous change that contributes to stress and creates problems. The story of my own first years of teaching shed some light on how I came to appreciate the importance of decreasing the amount of change teachers and students have to make. It shows the benefits for everyone when change is reduced.

MY EXPERIENCE AS A TEACHER

I taught mentally retarded children for three years. My first year was difficult, as it is for most teachers. Conversations with fellow first year teachers lead me to believe they were having the same types of problems I was having. The second year I went to a different school system. The special education department consisted of four classes.

Each child spent a total of eight years in the program because every child stayed in a room for two years. I had the ten and eleven year olds, and things went more smoothly that year. I was amazed at what just one year of experience can do, but I still did not think of myself as a good teacher.

At the end of the year, half of my class, my oldest students, were promoted to the next classroom, and I retained the younger students. In the fall I received some new students from the class below me. At the beginning of my third year of teaching, my class consisted half of returning students and half new ones. Since I still did not think of myself as a good teacher, I felt a little sorry for the students who would be having me two years in a row. But what I learned from this experience was a real eye opener to what students need and how they can be helped.

One day in the middle of the school year, I was sitting at my desk looking at the students and making a mental list of which ones caused me no problems, and which students were "difficult." The list of students who were "no problems" consisted exclusively of my eleven year olds -- the students I had retained from the previous year. A light bulb went off in my head. These eleven year olds were not easy because they were one year older! (The eleven year olds I had last year were not particularly easy!) These returning students were easy because they were returning students, period.

When you stop to think about it, is this surprising? The students knew me and they knew what I expected of them. They had learned how to function in the system I set up. In turn, I knew the students. I understood the limits of these students. I was able to give each of them work they could handle and that matched the way they learned. Since both the students and I had "worked things out between us," it follows that everyone functioned effectively.

It was the new students who gave me problems. These new students were not familiar with the way I explained things, and they did not know how I wanted assignments done. They also did not see the distinction I made between just normal, fun-loving playfulness, and which behavior I would not tolerate and would punish. Likewise, I did not understand them. I had no experience to guide me regarding what they could and could not do. I did not understand their specific learning patterns and styles. I had not yet discovered effective methods for them to encourage self discipline. In a nutshell, they had not figured me out and I had not figured them out.

It takes time for students to learn how to meet the expectations of a particular teacher, and it takes time for a teacher to really understand each student. If the student does not have any particular problems with school, he can function well, and there is no pressing need for the teacher to understand him. But when a child has a problem, it often is not until well into the school year that the teacher comes to truly understand the problem. Then it takes even more time to find an effective way of dealing with it. By this time the school year is almost over and the process starts all over again the following year. It is a frustrating situation for everyone, and little gets done to help the student.

Does my experience with mentally retarded children have any relevance to working with youngsters with emotional problems? Research tells us that although all retarded children do not have emotional problems, many of them do. They have a greater incidence of emotional problems than is found in the general population. Every teacher has a class containing children with emotional problems, but my classroom of retarded students had a higher percentage of youngsters with emotional problems than usual. The students I had for a second year were more comfortable themselves and were more comfortable for me to work with than they had been the first year I taught them. The system of retaining students for a second year worked to reduce stress for all of us. It allowed us to work more efficiently in an environment of mutual respect and trust.

Aside from all of this, there is another issue of equal importance: the emotional bonding that occurs between student and teacher. After spending an academic year with my students, I became attached to them and I am happy to say they became attached to me. Some of their cooperation came from a willingness to please me, arising from a realization that I liked them. This emotional bonding is as much a factor in the comfort level of the classroom as the fact that the children had lessons which matched their skills and style of learning. My experience taught me that children can function better in a school environment where there is an emotional bond between themselves and the teacher, but this bonding takes time to develop. In the years which followed, I heard other stories from teachers who echoed my experience.

After a fourth year of teaching elementary children, I became an instructor of psychology at the college level. Among the classes I taught were courses in child psychology, adolescent psychology, and educational psychology. During the summer school session, we had many graduate students -- classroom teachers coming to do advanced work. Often these classes had an equal number of older graduate students and younger undergraduates. In The King and I, there is the line saying that if you are a teacher, it is your students who will teach you. Teaching adolescent psychology to a number of junior high teachers is a very humbling experience, and I learned much more from them than they did from me.

THE STORY OF A JUNIOR HIGH TEACHER

One teacher said something that seems especially relevant here. He told me about his beginning years of teaching. During those years he was the seventh and eighth grade teacher in a four-room schoolhouse. In that setting he never had any problems with his students: he knew the students, the students knew him. He did not even have many problems with the new, incoming seventh graders each year. How was that so? He attributed it to four factors. First, the seventh graders were new to his classroom, but not totally new to him. They had some contact with him and knew him from interaction on the playground. Second, in normal conversation between the fifth and sixth graders and the seventh and eighth graders, incoming students picked up plenty of clues about what to expect when they got into the upper grades. Third, over the years he inevitably had students from the same family. The younger brothers and sisters would learn much of how things were done in Mr. X's room from the conversation around the dinner table. Fourth, the tradition of how things were done in his room were often learned by the seventh graders from a buddy in the neighborhood. For whatever reason or combination of factors, this teacher never had to deal with discipline problems when he taught in the four-room schoolhouse.

Then came "the consolidated school district." His school was closed, and he and the students were moved to the new junior high building. Now he had to deal with discipline problems! Same teacher, same type of school population, but no opportunity for him to develop a deep understanding of his students, learning patterns or problems; no opportunity for them to learn his methods or his expectations; and no time for emotional bonding to occur. This all added up to problems for both the teacher and the students, not to mention the parents who suffered right along with them.

This fine teacher had signed up for my adolescent psychology class in hopes of finding out more about that stage of life so he could cope more effectively with the problems he was seeing. But his own experience taught him more than I or any textbook could. It told him that the situation the seventh and eight graders were now in was more difficult to cope with than the stable classroom they had known. His life experience taught him that in a situation where students were less rooted, they acted less stable, and they had more problems.

SIMPLE ADJUSTMENTS TO EXISTING SCHOOLS

We can not turn back the clock and bring back four-room schoolhouses. No one would want to do this. I would, however, like to see parents, teachers, and students have some real choice in education which includes the opportunity to decrease changes. Although experienced teachers and administrators can undoubtedly think of other workable plans that are just as effective in reducing change and stress for teachers and students, here is one way I believe it could be done.

After the completion of kindergarten, parents would have the option of sending their child to a classroom that allows the child to have the same teacher for a number of years. What I envision is having a teacher teach first grade one year and then become the second grade teacher for that group the next year. The third grade teacher would take these students through third and fourth grades. Any special teaching methods that had been successful for a child with some sort of learning problem could be communicated between these teachers. Systems that were not successful, or that made things worse, could also be avoided by the third grade teacher.

Perhaps by the time the students got to fifth and sixth grades, they would be ready to have one teacher for half the day who had a special interest in language arts, social studies, and another teacher for the other half of the day who wanted to concentrate on math and science. These teachers would have the same students for two years in a row, but they would only teach half of the classes. Thus Mr. X could teach fifth grade language arts and social studies in the morning and sixth grade language arts and social studies in the afternoon. Mr. Y would teach sixth grade science and math in the morning and fifth grade science and math in the afternoon.

As students moved to junior high and perhaps even into senior high, there could be a few classrooms set aside for those students who choose the more self-contained approach. Students might merge with other students for some subjects, especially those requiring equipment like band, computer science, and physical education. However, they may instead wish to continue with their basic instructors for subjects like language arts, social studies, and math, in a self-contained setting. Students and their parents could, at specific times, have the option to either pull out of the self-contained system, or enter it.

This system of choice would allow the parents and children who like the current system of getting a new teacher each year of elementary school to continue to do so. However, in a large elementary school, with a number of rooms on each grade level, they could have some of the classes continue as they had in the past, while others would have this system. If, for example, half the parents want their child to have the same teacher for two years, then half of the classrooms would do this. The teachers who would most like to try this experiment in decreasing stress for themselves and their students would be the teachers who would have the same students two years in a row.

A few words of caution about this two-year system: All experienced teachers and administrators know that sometimes there are personality conflicts that naturally occur between particular teachers and students. When a child is going to have a teacher two years in a row, it is important to recognize when authentic personality conflicts occur, and arrange to move the child out of the classroom when necessary. I recall teaching one youngster who was a capable student and did not cause me any particular problem; I felt sorry for him, however, because I realized that I was not the best teacher for him. He would have been happier with someone else. When the moving of students is done in an environment where neither the teacher nor the student is blamed for a personality conflict, the switch can be done without any question of failure.

Second, there will be times in which teachers find themselves with an over-abundance of "problem" students. Keeping all those youngsters in one classroom for one year, much less two, is not in anyone's best interest. There must be some flexibility about equal distribution of students with special needs.

In junior and senior high the current system of a new teacher each hour can be retained for all the students and parents who like the system. I do not wish to suggest that we should fix something that is not broken. The present system should be retained for the many students and teachers who are comfortable with it. For many other students, the more stable system of a self-contained class with some merger at various hours can be helpful. Often young people feel they are worthless. They view themselves as little fish in a big pond. We can not throw away all the large schools and build smaller ones, but we can develop a number of smaller environments within a larger system. These systems would be based on having the same teacher for a number of years: someone who understands, someone who really cares, and someone who is cared about in return.

Chapter 8

If I Ran a School

One night I asked myself, "What would you do to meet the requirements of young people with special needs if you were the principal of a school?" To answer that question realistically, I envisioned a school with little or no money for any type of special program. This is the plan that emerged.

The screening for youngsters with dyslexia would be done by simply asking the teachers to jot down a list of the students in their classes who had difficulty with reading and spelling. This produces a list of students with reading blindness, as well as many other learning problems. Since the goal is to support all students who need help, it does not harm anyone if the original screening and subsequent tutoring goes to youngsters with a wide range of problems.

All children with reading and spelling problems would be offered the assistance of a tutor/buddy. This fellow student would assist that youngster with their reading and spelling assignment by using the system of presenting questions, corrective feedback, and contingent social reinforcement mentioned earlier. When time permitted, the tutor would also work on phonics games with that student.

The screening for ADHD would be done by simply asking the teachers to jot down a list of students in their class who had difficulty getting their work done on time. This too would produce a list of students with a variety of problems other than ADHD. Remember, the goal is not to exclude students who do not qualify under rigid guidelines. The goal is to be helpful to all students who need it.

All children with problems getting their assignment completed would be offered the assistance of the same type of buddy/tutor who would help with all of their subjects. They may have a different tutor each day of the week or a different tutor for each subject. No one fellow student can be expected to help that child every day for all of the assignments, but several students can share the tutoring. These students will use the same system of presenting questions, corrective feedback, and contingent social reinforcement described earlier.

As principal, I would see my job as needing to be supportive of the parents of these youngsters and of their teachers. If I only focus on the students and fail to meet the needs of the most important adults in the children's lives, I will ultimately fail these children. Consequently, after the children have been screened for learning problems, I would write to their parents. The letter would be my best effort to be both supportive and informative. It may go something like this.

Dear Mr. and Mrs. Jones,

This year I asked the teachers to give me a list of the students in their classes who have difficulty (use one -- reading and spelling OR getting their work done). Mrs. X (insert name of teacher) indicates that Johnny (name of student) is having some difficulty.

This may or may not be an indication of a learning problem. One simple approach to meeting his needs is to have other students help him with his assignments. If you are interested in having us try this, please return the enclosed permission slip.

Also enclosed is a list of characteristics of students with learning problems. In the months and years ahead, you may wish to look over your child's work and give us your opinion about whether or not you think that he has a learning problem. It is important to know that a learning problem is neither the fault of the child nor the parents. Although the parents and the child have not caused this problem, much can be done by both to learn to cope with it. If you are ever interested in discussing this with me and/or meeting with other parents whose children may also have a learning problem, please contact the office at 123-4567 (insert correct phone number).

Sincerely,

Ms. Y
Principal

The parents who respond to this letter can be guided into the development of a support group. A teacher particularly interested in working with parents or the principal may need to attend the first meetings; however, in any group there are participants with natural leadership ability who will soon be able to take over facilitating the group. Ideally, the meeting will be on a shared or rotating basis so that every member has a sense of ownership that comes naturally if they are allowed to have full participation in the support group.

There will likely be one group for parents of youngsters with dyslexia whose focus is on learning more about the condition and how to cope with it. They may want information about the Orton Society which is dedicated to helping people with reading blindness.

The parents of youngsters with ADHD will want to share their experiences with medication, learn contingency management skills, learn about the self-control training system, and form the social skills and athletics clubs that are helpful for their children.

Although these groups will want to meet separately much of the time, they may want to meet together sometimes because:

1. *young people with dyslexia may also have ADHD*

2. *depression is common for young people with dyslexia and youngsters with ADHD*

3. *anxiety is often found in youngsters with dyslexia, as well as ADHD*

4. *parents whose child has any type of learning problem are interested in finding out what other parents face and how they cope with it.*

It may be helpful to have both groups meet together at least three times a year to learn about the symptoms of depression and anxiety as they manifest in young people, and to share their experiences with their child. These common meetings would also help to prevent unnecessary separation between families who experience a common problem: the pain of seeing their child struggle so hard to do what so many other children do easily.

As a principal, I would do my best to be supportive of the classroom teacher. Instead of giving them more and more to do, I would attempt to streamline or simplify tasks whenever possible. Our current system requires a burdensome amount of paperwork for students with special needs. If I could do anything to simplify the system of meeting regulatory requirements by emphasizing a streamlined, common sense approach to this paperwork, I would do this:

Every teacher will have some children in his class with difficulties, but if a teacher has a significantly larger number of students with special needs as compared to the other teachers in the building, that teacher could be given the option of having some of the students moved to another classroom. This would be done in a no-fault, no-favoritism manner by informing the parents of the situation and inviting them to witness the "pulling the names out of a hat" ceremony when a child or a number of children need to be moved.

I believe the biggest contribution towards reducing the number of problems teachers have to cope with is to allow them to keep their students for at least two grades. In some school systems where the early elementary school consists of students Kindergarten through Third Grade, teachers are keeping their pupils for the full three years after kindergarten. Reports are that the teacher and parents like the system a great deal. It is comfortable for everyone because it allows the student and teachers to be efficient and enjoy the results of their efforts.

The system described here for helping students with special needs is not perfect, but it also does not cost any money, would not cause harm, and probably would do much good. No one is perfect; not the child, the parent, the teacher, or the administrators. But it is my firm belief that all of us want to do our best to help each other. This system is just one common sense approach that would allow us to do that.

Chapter 9

Respecting Individual Differences

"The need for educational tests and policy measures to identify, accommodate, and serve differentially specialized forms of individual potential is becoming increasingly evident." These words were spoken by Roger Speary, winner of the Nobel Prize for his famous work on the right and left hemispheres of the brain. His remarks underscore the importance of respecting individual differences. As we begin to appreciate the great variability in the biological nature of the human brain, we wonder if it is reasonable to expect uniform performance from young people.

Many otherwise talented young people may not be well suited for typical classroom instruction. It is important to remember that Thomas Edison spent less than one year in a classroom. His mother sent him to first grade, but when he did not seem to profit from the experience, she kept him home and taught him herself. She used his natural interests and his own particular way of learning as a guide on how to teach him.

HISTORICAL PERSPECTIVE

Ever since World War II, there has been accelerating emphasis on formal education. The GI Bill served a double purpose of giving veterans further training while keeping them out of the job market while the country readjusted to a post-war economy. The launch of Sputnik, and the fear it engendered that the Soviet Union was ahead of us, placed renewed emphasis on formal training in a classroom setting and pressure to improve skills in reading, science, and math. The cold war's emphasis on competition rather than cooperation was echoed in the classroom. The rise of automation, the reduction in manual labor, and today's use of computers all have fueled the focus on language skills and the ability to concentrate.

In our attempt to encourage young people to acquire marketable skills necessary to compete in today's society, we may be inadvertently sending the message to those young people whose brains are not biologically designed to acquire language easily or to concentrate on academic tasks that they are failures, or even bad people.

In our efforts to encourage academic skill, we may neglect to communicate to children that they may be talented but not in the area of doing their school work. Learning-disabled students need support throughout school years by fellow classmates, teachers, and parents who understand the biological nature of their condition.

When I consider man's long history as a species on this planet and the relatively short time we have had high rates of literacy, I realize that books for mass distribution are relatively new inventions. Up to the 19th Century, few people learned how to read, write, or calculate numbers. Survival was based on the ability to hunt or raise food, and build shelters. Man has been on this planet for thousands of years and it is just recently that we have emphasized the acquisition of high level academic skills as necessary for a large segment of our population. We may be accidentally and quite inaccurately making some people feel "less than a person" if they are unable to acquire these skills.

My own father is a good example of a successful man who rejected academic training but was not made to feel he was bad or stupid. Born in 1902, he stayed in school until sometime in 5th grade, when he decided that he had had enough of formal education. His rejection of school in 1912 was not a problem for his family or his community. He was a bright, energetic youngster for whom farm life offered many opportunities to work and to learn. Formal education had given him sufficient reading skills to handle a newspaper -- the only written material that interested him. The confinement of the quiet classroom routine held little charm for him when compared to the life he enjoyed at home.

My father's interests were basically the same as Ben's. He liked to do manual work. He could have made a good living in the building trades as a mason, but preferried being his own boss, so he purchased a dairy farm. Well-respected in his community, his non-completion of elementary school did not in the least affect his life as an adult. My father's life is an important example for me because it is easy to forget that it was not so very long ago that formal education was mostly irrelevant to a large segment of our population.

Today's children do not have the same opportunity my father had. They are compelled to conform to the demands of the unnatural environment of a classroom. Man is a creature who adapts easily to a number of different environments. Many youngsters have a brain whose anatomy and chemistry allows them to function quite well in the artificial environment of the schoolroom. But some youngster's biology is not well suited for that setting.

In addition to what we call learning disabilities, some youngsters have other health problems, or have a home environment fraught with the stress of financial instability, and/or problems created by one or more difficulties the parents have. These youngsters may be ill-equipped to meet the artificial demands of learning the three R's. This book is focused on dyslexia and ADHD, but the programs it suggests can be beneficial to all young people who need support for any reason.

CONTINUED PROBLEMS DESPITE BEST EFFORTS

When thinking about the importance of meeting the needs of individual differences, it is essential to keep in mind that, despite the very best efforts of the most talented and compassionate teachers, the most loving and wise parents, some children will still have great problems with school. Even when the most dedicated parents and teachers work together to diligently provide learning experiences that emphasize the child's talents and interests, some youngsters with serious problems will still show signs of distress.

1. Low self-esteem is a symptom of depression.

If the child's depression is biologically based, he will suffer from low self-esteem no matter how supportive the environment or how often he is provided with tasks that produce success.

2. Oppositional defiance is a condition in which the child opposes what a parent or teacher suggests.

Even though the activity is carefully designed to meet the child's individual needs and takes advantage of the child's interests, the youngster with this condition will still object to doing his assignments.

3. Anger and irritability are common symptoms of depression in children.

The child may be angry at teachers, parents, and/or peers, even though to the casual observer there is no logical reason for anger. Irritability may make them difficult to get along with, despite everyone's willingness to help them and make allowances for the problems.

4. ADHD children are impulsive.

No matter how often parents and teachers tell them to think before they act, planning ahead and seeing the consequence of their actions is not natural for them. Their impulsivity is chronic.

5. *The depression which frequently accompanies this condition can result from becoming disheartened as children struggle to cope with their learning disability, but depression can also be biologically based.*

In my own son's case, I was later able to identify symptoms of his condition (eating problems and sleeping problems) that were present in infancy -- long before he entered a classroom.

All that any of us can expect of ourselves is that :

1. *we attempt to understand the deficit the child has. (Ben once said to me, "You don't know what it means to me to have someone who understands."),*

2. *we make an attempt to give the child tasks they can realistically do with their current academic skills and with their level of ability to concentrate, and*

3. *we encourage peers and other readily available support systems which allow the child to feel that he is not alone.*

TYPICAL DISTRIBUTION PATTERNS: SEVERE CASES ARE RARE

What are the chances that any child with dyslexia or ADHD will learn to cope with his disability? It depends on how severe the condition is. Many human variables fall into a typical distribution pattern. This type of pattern means that most people are similar to each other, and the incidence of cases that are in either extreme of what is typical are few in number. An example of this is height. Most adult males are 5'8 to 5'10 inches tall. 6' is tall but not rare. As height gets higher, the numbers of persons who are that tall are few. The same is true of being short. 5'6" is relatively short but not uncommon. The further one's height is from that "norm," the rarer it is.

It is likely that learning disabilities and depressive illness have this same type of distribution. Most people with learning disabilities have a mild case. The future of these people is far from bleak. Like my father, I was able to become a successful independent business person. Dr. Drake Duane mentioned in his lecture on learning disabilities that the chances of overcoming a disability are strong if the child has a number of these factors:

1. *a mild case*

2. *early and appropriate intervention*

3. *high intelligence*

4. *some problem-solving skills*

5. *a stable home*

6. *good rapport with others (social skills)*

7. *strong socio-economic background*

8. *something that goes well in his life, that can give him status among peers (e.g. a talent in music, art, athletics, drama, etc.)*

The majority of people with depression also have a mild or moderate case. Programs designed to correct the symptoms of depression (the cognitive errors and problems with interpersonal relationships) have proved to be successful therapy for alleviating this condition.

AVOIDING LEARNED HELPLESSNESS

Besides treating depression when it occurs, it is essential that we do not inadvertently create an environment that may cause children to become disheartened -- learned helplessness. Dr. Gold has shown how this occurs in the laboratory with animals as subjects.

Apparent depression can be experimentally induced in rats. Yoke two rats together in a cage with a wheel on one wall. Give control of the wheel only to the rat on the left. Now give them both an identical electric shock. The shock will stop when the rat on the left turns the wheel. Although the shock begins and ends at the same time for both rats, it is the rat on the right who gets depressed. This rat had no control over what happened to it, and ends up giving up on life -- the learned helplessness effect. Now put it in a situation where it will be able to escape the shock, and it will not be able to learn how. It will eat less, lose weight, develop stomach problems, and be less aggressive.

Learning helplessness has been proposed as one model for human depression as well. Disadvantaged and/or scapegoated segments of society are at risk. Family dynamics can produce this kind of depression in the child who learns through the horrors of experience that she or he is helpless and unable to control abuse; or, more subtly, in the family member, adult or child, who is consistently deprived of respect and power. (Gold, 1987 The Good News About Depression)

Towards the end of Ben's fifth grade year, when he was feeling so disheartened about not doing well in school and I tried to comfort him by telling him that I thought he had a learning disability, he said, "Maybe my problem is that I am just lazy." What Ben did not fully understand was the research of the psychology of motivation. All people are motivated to do something if what they are expected to do is a desirable goal, and it can be successfully achieved with a reasonable amount of effort.

Academic skill has such high status in our culture that virtually every child, adolescent and adult sees the acquisition of these skills as a desirable goal. In other words, every student wants to learn. But if students can not succeed with a reasonable amount of effort, or cannot seem to succeed on their own no matter how hard they try, they will stop trying. This is not laziness, this is just common sense. Evidence for this abounds in the research done in psychology and education, and is true in animal studies as well as on people.

If students are to continue to keep trying, they must have assignments that they can succeed in accomplishing, and the tasks must not be too difficult.

ALL LEARNING PROBLEMS SHOULD BE TAKEN SERIOUSLY

All children and their individual problems need to be taken seriously. Whether it is dyslexia, ADHD, biologically created depressive illness, financial stress, parents with health or other problems, a serious loss, or any of a wide range of problems; these students all need help. Giving parents, teachers, and the child the power to choose to be involved in a generic program that can provide mutual help and support is one feasible way to include anyone who wishes to be involved. Most persons with learning disabilities and depression, as well as those with other stressors, can be helped. The first step is to take the problems seriously!

Works Cited

Barkley, R.A. Attention deficit disorder with hyperactivity. New York: Guilford Press

Braswell, L., Bloomquist, M., & Pederson, S. (1991). ADHD: A guide to understanding and helping children with attention deficit hyperactivity disorder in school settings. Minneapolis: University of Minnesota Press.

Duane, D.D. (1991). Biological foundations of learning disabilities. Neuropsychological Foundations of Learning Disabilities. Academic Press.

Durlak, J.A. (1985). Primary prevention of school maladjustment. Journal of Consulting & Clinical Psychology, 53, 623-630.

Gold, M.S. (1987). The good news about depression. New York: Bantam Books.

Teeter, P.A. (1991). Attention deficit hyperactivity disorder: A psychoeducational paradigm. School Psychology Review. 20:2, 266-280.

Useful information on suicide. (1986). U.S. Department of Health and Human Services. National Institute of Mental Health.

Veninga, R.L. (1985). A gift of hope: How we survive our tragedies. New York: Ballantine Books

Further References

Adolescent stress and depression. (1986). Teens in distress. University of Minnesota: Minnesota Extension Service.

Burns, D.D., MD (1980). Feeling good: The new mood therapy. New York: Signet Books.

Elmer-Dewitt, P. (1992, July 6). Depression: The growing role of drug therapies. Time, pp. 57-59.

Fieve, F.R., MD (1975). Moodswings. New York: Bantam Books.

Fishman, K.D. (1991, June). Therapy for children. The Atlantic Monthly, pp. 47-69.

Goode, E. (1990, March 5). Beating depression. U.S. News & World Report, pp. 48-55.

Hewett, J.H. (1980). After suicide. Philadelphia, Pennsylvania: The Westminster Press.

Hoberman, H.M., Ph.D. (1989). "Completed suicide in children and adolescents: A review." In B.D. Garfinkel (Ed.), Adolescent suicide: Recognition, treatment, and prevention. New York: Haworth.

Klerman, G., Weissman, M., Rounsaville, B., & Chevron, E. (1984). Interpersonal psychotherapy of depression. New York: Basic Books, Inc.

Larson, D.E., MD (Ed.). (1990). Mayo Clinic family health book. New York: William Morrow and Company, Inc.

McKay, M. & Fanning, P. (1987). Self esteem. Oakland, California: New Harbinger Publications.

McKnew, D.H., Cytryn, L., & Yahraes, H. (1983). Why isn't Johnny crying? Coping with depression in children. New York: Norton & Company.

Moss, R.A. (1990). Why Johnny can't concentrate: Coping with attention deficit problems. New York: Bantam Books.

Papolos, D., and Papolos, J. (1992). Overcoming depression. New York: Harper Perennial.

Popper, C., MD (1989). Diagnosing bipolar vs. ADHD. American Academy of Child and Adolescent Psychaitry News. Washington DC

Sargent, M. (a). Depressive illnesses: Treatment brings new hope. U.S. Department of Health and Human Services. National Institute of Mental Health.

Sargent, M. (b). Helping the depressed person get treatment. U.S. Department of Health and Human Services. National Institute of Mental Health.

Sarnoff Schiff, H. (1977). The bereaved parent. New York: Penguin Books.

Sheehan, D.V. (1983). The anxiety disease. New York: Bantam Books.

Supporting distressed young people. (1985). Teens in distress. University of Minnesota: Minnesota Extension Service.

Supporting young people following a suicide. (1986) Teens in distress. University of Minnesota: Minnesota Extension Service.

Teen suicide. (1985). Teens in distress. University of Minnesota: Minnesota Extension Service.

Useful information on suicide. (1986). U.S. Department of Health and Human Services. National Institute of Mental Health.

Veninga, R.L. (1985). A gift of hope: How we survive our tragedies. New York: Ballantine Books

Index

—A—

achievement, 16, 32, 35, 55, 69, 70, 71, 72
ADHD, 1, 5, 6, 7, 2, 3, 5, 6, 7, 9, 12, 13, 14, 17, 21, 24, 26, 28, 36, 37, 38, 39, 40, 41, 42, 45, 46, 47, 48, 49, 50, 51, 53, 54, 55, 56, 58, 59, 60, 61, 62, 63, 64, 65, 66, 67, 68, 69, 73, 74, 75, 76, 77, 78, 83, 84, 85, 86, 87, 88, 89, 93, 98, 99, 100, 111, 114, 120, 121, 122, 126, 127, 129
adolescence, 53
adolescent, 25, 53, 105, 106, 125
aggressive, 41, 125
Aikido, 61
anatomy, 20, 42, 43, 44, 45, 83, 120
antidepressant, 20, 22, 49
anxiety, 2, 6, 28, 33, 49, 50, 114, 115, 129
aptitude, 16, 70, 71
asset, 34, 39, 90
assignment, 11, 14, 76, 83, 111, 112
associations, 10
athletic, 34
attention, 2, 3, 6, 9, 10, 11, 15, 16, 18, 19, 20, 22, 27, 28, 41, 45, 46, 49, 54, 64, 65, 66, 68, 71, 75, 76, 79, 83, 87, 88, 98, 127, 129
attention span, 18, 49, 65
attitude, 94
autism, 67
autopsy, 44

—B—

band, 23, 25, 26, 40, 83, 108
benefits, 59, 91, 92, 93, 96, 101
Bloomquist, 46, 51, 52, 127
bonding, 104, 106
Bradley, 50
brain chemistry, 10, 45, 83
Braswell, 46, 51, 127
Buddy, 6, 58
buses, 88

—C—

Ch.A.D.D., 55, 57
challenge, 4, 53, 58, 87, 98
chemistry, 10, 42, 45, 83, 120
Christmas, 84
chronic, 67, 88, 121
classroom, 5, 11, 17, 21, 31, 35, 36, 48, 54, 57, 58, 64, 69, 70, 71, 73, 74, 76, 80, 82, 83, 84, 87, 89, 96, 97, 98, 100, 102, 104, 105, 106, 107, 109, 115, 117, 118, 119, 122
club, 34, 41, 57, 59, 60, 61
cognitive therapy, 62
college, 66, 105
competition, 35, 95, 96, 97, 118
comprehend, 13
computer, 15, 20, 23, 25, 75, 108
concentration, 9, 25, 36, 64, 66, 69, 71, 75, 88, 98
conference, 19, 20, 21, 22, 23, 72
consequences, 51, 52, 59, 65, 75, 77, 78
consolidated, 106
contingent, 97, 111, 112
cooperation, 4, 5, 23, 95, 96, 104, 118
coordination, 18
cortical surface, 44
Cylert, 48, 49
cynical, 92

—D—

destruction, 87
Dexedrine, 48, 49
diabetic, 47, 67
diagnosed, 45, 67, 78, 85, 86, 87
difference, 35, 41, 71, 75, 88, 94
directions, 3, 76
disheartened, 1, 122, 124, 125
disruptive, 49, 83, 86, 88
distracted, 18, 46, 71, 80, 83
drowns, 84
Duane, 9, 19, 44, 123, 127
dyslexia, 1, 2, 3, 27, 28, 32, 41, 42, 43, 44, 45, 73, 83, 111, 114, 120, 122, 126
dysplasia, 44

—E—

eating, 67, 85, 122
Edison, 117
education, 6, 20, 57, 61, 62, 101, 107, 108, 117, 119, 125
efficient, 10, 95, 98, 99, 116
energetic, 39, 119
environment, 9, 14, 69, 74, 95, 96, 104, 109, 119, 120, 121, 124
evaluation, 7, 16, 21, 22, 53, 54, 70, 72, 73, 82
expectations, 10, 103, 106
experience, 23, 34, 40, 41, 46, 66, 72, 73, 76, 90, 92, 93, 94, 101, 102, 103, 104, 105, 106, 114, 115, 117, 125

—F—

feedback, 41, 97, 111, 112
females, 45
fidgets, 80
Florida, 84
foreign language, 1, 36, 42, 43
frontal, 46

—G—

Galaburda, 43
girls, 35, 45, 47
gym, 61, 65
gymnastics, 61

—H—

habit, 11
habits, 3, 10, 21, 67
hallways, 88
handicapped, 54, 55
handwriting, 12, 20, 23, 49
helpful, 4, 5, 10, 12, 20, 22, 23, 26, 28, 49, 51, 53, 57, 90, 93, 110, 112, 114, 115, 135
helplessness, 1, 2, 5, 36, 124, 125
hemisphere, 43, 44
hemispheres, 43, 44, 117
high school, 16, 24, 41, 42, 66
hope, 4, 7, 16, 28, 31, 36, 63, 127, 129
hopelessness, 1, 2, 5, 36
horses, 40
humiliated, 30, 37

—I—

impulsivity, 3, 24, 25, 49, 51, 61, 65, 66, 68, 69, 76, 80, 86, 121
inappropriate, 18, 41, 75, 80
inattention, 61, 65, 66, 68, 69, 76, 79, 83, 86
inconsistent, 19, 73, 74, 79, 80
instruction, 25, 50, 51, 117
intelligence, 28, 37, 44, 46, 50, 67, 71, 88, 96, 123
interpersonal skills, 41, 62
intonation, 13

—K—

karate, 61, 75
kindergarten, 7, 107, 116

—L—

leadership, 35, 41, 113
lecture, 20, 123
left side, 42, 43, 44
lessons, 8, 24, 59, 61, 92, 93, 104
Loss, 135

—M—

manipulative, 9, 10
martial arts, 40, 60, 61, 76
math, 1, 13, 15, 16, 25, 26, 33, 38, 70, 72, 74, 82, 83, 99, 108, 118
Mayo Clinic, 2, 19, 21, 22, 23, 128
meaningless, 90
medication, 20, 22, 26, 47, 48, 49, 67, 114
memorizing, 30
messy, 12, 19, 20, 37
migrated, 43
misbehavior, 9
motivational, 3

—N—

neurons, 44
neurotransmitters, 10, 45, 47, 68, 85
nightmare, 15

—O—

observation, 46, 69, 72, 82, 83
overactivity, 3, 48, 61, 65, 66

—P—

Parker, 55
peer, 49, 91, 92, 93, 94, 96, 97, 98
percentile, 22
performance, 10, 11, 17, 19, 22, 30, 32, 34, 37, 53, 63, 64, 69, 70, 71, 72, 73, 83, 117
phonics, 31, 36, 38, 111
physical activities, 57, 61
playgrounds, 88
prefrontal, 46
psychology, 6, 105, 106, 125

—R—

racquetball, 60, 61, 75
reading, 1, 2, 3, 9, 13, 15, 16, 22, 25, 29, 30, 31, 32, 33, 35, 36, 38, 39, 40, 41, 42, 43, 45, 63, 70, 72, 83, 91, 92, 93, 94, 99, 111, 112, 114, 118, 119
reassurance, 39
reinforcement, 9, 10, 50, 54, 57, 78, 97, 111, 112
rejection, 41, 119
researchers, 47, 65, 68
respect, 34, 63, 74, 104, 125
retain, 13
retaining, 96, 104
reverses, 18
right side, 43, 44
Ritalin, 48, 49

—S—

school, 1, 4, 7, 8, 9, 10, 11, 13, 14, 15, 16, 17, 20, 21, 22, 23, 24, 25, 26, 27, 28, 30, 31, 32, 33, 34, 35, 37, 38, 39, 40, 41, 42, 46, 47, 48, 53, 57, 59, 60, 61, 62, 64, 65, 66, 67, 69, 72, 73, 74, 77, 78, 80, 81, 83, 84, 85,

86, 87, 88, 90, 94, 98, 100, 101, 102, 103, 104, 105, 106, 108, 110, 111, 116, 118, 119, 120, 125, 127
schoolwork, 15, 79, 80
science, 1, 23, 108, 118
sensitive, 2, 32, 38, 93
Shaming, 77
sleeping, 85, 122
sloppy, 37
special education, 20, 101
speech, 12, 19, 20, 42, 43
spelling, 3, 20, 22, 23, 25, 32, 33, 35, 36, 39, 41, 42, 43, 82, 83, 99, 111, 112
standardized, 69, 71
stress, 4, 5, 57, 89, 96, 101, 104, 107, 109, 120, 126, 128
success, 101, 121
suicide, 1, 2, 5, 6, 35, 42, 127, 128, 129
support, 5, 14, 26, 28, 38, 39, 41, 55, 56, 57, 58, 60, 61, 73, 96, 97, 111, 113, 118, 120, 122, 126
swimmer, 40
sympathetic, 55, 95

—T—

talking, 15, 43, 82, 83
tasks, 8, 10, 20, 37, 46, 76, 79, 80, 89, 94, 115, 118, 121, 122, 126
teacher, 1, 2, 6, 8, 9, 10, 11, 12, 13, 17, 19, 21, 23, 24, 25, 26, 29, 30, 31, 32, 33, 35, 38, 49, 54,
57, 58, 60, 65, 66, 70, 71, 72, 73, 74, 82, 83, 87, 88, 89, 91, 94, 97, 98, 99, 100, 101, 102, 103, 104, 105, 106, 107, 108, 109, 112, 113, 115, 116, 121
temporal lobe, 43
test, 17, 21, 32, 33, 35, 67, 69, 70, 71, 76
testosterone, 44
toddlers, 65
Token, 54
Tragedy, 136
transportation, 60
trust, 104
trusted, 87
tutor, 12, 17, 21, 23, 25, 73, 92, 93, 99, 111, 112
tutoring, 7, 17, 22, 26, 91, 92, 93, 95, 96, 97, 98, 111, 112
TV, 8

—V—

vacation, 84

—W—

Wellbutrin, 49
work habits, 3, 10, 21
worthless, 90, 110

—Y—

YMCA, 61

ABOUT THE AUTHOR

Trudy Carlson never intended to write this book. Ben's death made her put aside her other writing in order to tell the story of his life. She wanted to record everything about the problems she observed during the various stages of his life, all the things she did to help him, and the attempt to obtain treatment for his condition.

As she worked she discovered she had four separate topics. The first became the book, The Suicide of My Son: A Story of Childhood Depression. This is now also published as two separate works: Ben's Story and Depression in the Young.

Learning Disabilities: How to Recognize & Manage Learning & Behavioral Problems in Children contrasts Ben's ADD (Attention Deficit Disorder) with her own personal struggle with a mild case of dyslexia. She explains why she was able to manage her problem and why Ben's was overwhelming.

Tragedy, Finding a Hidden Meaning: How to Transform the Tragedies in Your Life into Personal Growth, explores the personal and spiritual growth that can emerge from loss. "Meaning makes most things endurable, perhaps everything."

Suicide Survivors Handbook: A Guide for the Bereaved and Those Who Wish to Help Them, deals with the major issues confronting the survivor. It also gives a wealth of suggestions on what is most helpful during recovery from grief.

ORDER FORM

Telephone orders: Call Toll Free: **1-800-296-7163**
Please have your Visa or MasterCard number ready
For mail orders make checks payable to:: **Benline Press,**
118 N. 60th Ave E., Duluth, MN. 55804.

Please send the following books. I understand that I may return any books for a full refund -- for any reason, no questions asked.

Suicide Survivors' Handbook: A Guide to the Bereaved and
Those Who Wish to Help Them $14.95 _____

The Suicide of My Son: A Story of Childhood Depression
                                     $16.95 _____

Tragedy: Finding a Hidden Meaning -- How to Transform
the Tragedies in Your Life into Personal Growth
                                     $14.95 _____

Learning Disabilities: How to Recognize and Manage,
Learning and Behavioral Problems in Children
                                     $14.95 _____
Sales Tax: Add 6.5% for books shipped to Minnesota _____

Shipping: Book Rate: $2.00 for the first book and 75 cents for each additional book. (Surface shipping may take three to four weeks)   Airmail: $3.50 per book
                        Total   _____

Payment: __ check __ credit card
Card Number:_____
Name on card:_____
Exp. Date _____/_____